Winston Churchill

Statesman of the Century

Robin H. Neillands

'Neillands' power as a writer and historian makes Churchill's life relevant for twenty-first century readers interested in the key events of the twentieth century...In clear, concise language, Neillands tells the story of Churchill's preparation for greatness.'

–From the Foreword by Professor Robert Berlin

ALSO BY ROBIN NEILLANDS

Cold Spring Press

P.O. Box 284
Cold Spring Harbor, NY 11724
E-mail: Jopenroad@aol.com

This book is dedicated to Dr. Christine Jackson and Dr. Tom Buchanan of Oxford University. They got me started on all this.

PUBLISHER'S NOTE

We have not Americanized the spelling in this book, so you will see throughout the British spelling (e.g., *rigour* instead of rigor) in keeping with the author's voice and style.

Winston Churchill

Statesman of the Century

Robin H. Neillands

Cold Spring Press

Contents

Foreword

Winston Churchill: Statesman of the Century

To the British public, Winston Churchill is the Greatest Briton of all time. In 2002 the British Broadcast Corporation conducted a nationwide poll to find 'The Greatest Briton of Them All.' With over a million people voting Churchill won with 28.1 percent. By comparison, Shakespeare earned 6.8 percent and still made the top ten. If a similar poll were to be taken in America of famous Britons, surely Winston Churchill would rank number one. His face, figure, voice and commanding appearance are widely recognized. His image is one of greatness.

What made Churchill great? What attributes of personality, character, wisdom and knowledge and what personal experiences produced this Great Briton? Robin Neillands, in this masterful, succinct biography, establishes the basis for Churchill's achievements and lasting fame. Based on the most recent studies and his own historical exploration, Neillands gives us an understanding of Churchill's life set in the context of modern British history. Neillands goes beyond standard biography to explain in a sprightly style how Churchill became the 'greatest statesman of the 20th century.'

In a short, highly readable, literate biography Neillands portrays the living Churchill. His troubled relationship with his father, his education at Harrow and Sandhurst, his first visit to the United States in the 1890's, his military service and his emergence as a politician are all described and explained. Neillands' Churchill is a complex person, not a caricature. Neillands reveals and explains Churchill's many personas: soldier, horseman, war hero, journalist, author, historian, husband, public speaker, politician, parliamentarian, painter, national and world leader, and, to Neillands most significant—statesman. Churchill was amazingly energetic, both physically and intellectually. He developed his powers for selfish and patriotic reasons. His workdays were long. His pace daunting to most men, his mind was complex and his actions significant. Neillands' power as a writer and historian makes Churchill's life relevant for twenty-first century readers interested in the key events of the twentieth century.

Churchill could not have become the 'greatest statesman of the 20th century' without having mastered the skills necessary to lead his nation and the Allies prior to World War II. Churchill personally experienced combat in Cuba, Sudan, India, South Africa and the Western Front in France during World War I. He served fifty years as a member of the British Parliament. He was First Lord of the Admiralty and Minister of Munitions in World War I and spent much of the Interwar period (1918-1939), known as his 'wilderness years,' preparing himself and his nation for the life and death struggle ahead. In clear, concise language, Neillands tells the story of Churchill's preparation for greatness.

Churchill realized long before most other politicians and the British public that warfare had changed since World War I and that Germany was a threat to Great Britain; he knew that appeasement was not a sound policy. When World War II began, Churchill returned as First Lord of the Admiralty. Even before becoming Prime Minister in 1940 he began his extensive communication with United States President Franklin D. Roosevelt. Churchill's wartime leadership as Prime Minister from 1940 to 1945 was the pinnacle of his achievement as statesman.

Robin Neillands' vast knowledge of World War II is encapsulated here and seen from a Churchillian view. Neillands gives new perspective to the Battle of France, Dunkirk, the Battle of Britain, fighting in the Western Desert, the Battle of the Atlantic, the Air War, D-Day and the final victory over Nazism. From the founding of the Atlantic Charter to Churchill's 'Iron Curtain' speech in Fulton, Missouri, Neillands never loses sight of the Alliance point of view and of the diplomatic and political environment that Churchill worked in and shaped.

Winston Churchill: Statesman of the Century is an apt title for this fresh and convincing biography. There could be no greater subject for the first volume in the Cold Spring Press Great Leaders Biography series.

Professor Robert H. Berlin
School of Advanced Military Studies
U.S. Army Command and General Staff College
Fort Leavenworth, Kansas

Preface

According to one recent estimate some 500 books about Winston S. Churchill have been published since his death in 1965 – that's about 10 a year – and more are being published all the time. As I write these lines, I have before me an Australian paper reviewing another three recently published works on Winston Churchill, and in the face of this biographical blizzard two questions arise: why another book about Churchill, and what is there left to say?

Two points need to be made about this book. First it is not very long. Roy Jenkins' recent (2001) biography of Churchill offers a massive 1,000 pages and many other books on Churchill are as long or longer; Martin Gilbert's *Churchill: A Life,* published in 1991, weighs in at a formidable 1,045 pages. Both these books are excellent but not every reader wants to tackle such big books as biographical works of first instance, and it is to those people – and to those whom Winston Churchill, forty years after his death, is someone they have only vaguely heard of – that this particular book is directed.

To answer the first question therefore, this book aims to compress Churchill's long and active life into a short, relevant and entertaining whole, without sacrificing any of the essential points or dramatic incidents. Second, it will, I hope, explain to the modern reader who Churchill was, where he came from, what he did to attract such enduring and extensive attention – and how he came to be the man he was, a point that many biographies somehow manage to overlook.

Churchill's life is as remarkable as the man himself – born in the High Victorian Age, going to the wars on horseback, fighting Afghan tribesmen with a sabre – and living into the era of the atomic bomb. He spanned an entire age, and provided what little it had of glory. All books on Churchill make the point that he was a great man. This book explains the course of events and the quirks of character that *made* him a great man – in my view, *the* statesman of the past century – and why his life therefore provides useful lessons for later generations.

Churchill became great; he was not born that way. Indeed, until the age of 18 he was regarded, even by his father, as a total failure. In so far as this attempt to explain Churchill's rise to fame is successful – and you, the reader, must be the judge of that – it will answer the second question raised in the first paragraph above: what there is left to say about Winston Churchill?

The short answer to that question is – plenty. Winston Churchill's life is a rich tapestry. Almost everything the biographer could desire can be found there; colour, adventure, connections, danger, triumph, disaster, war, peace, good men, tyrants, Kings and Queens, Presidents and Prime Ministers, faith and betrayal, love and hate, art and history ... the reader or writer who cannot find something new and instructive in studying the life of Winston Spencer Churchill must be a very dull dog indeed. Churchill as a biographical subject is fascinating, but not easy.

The great paradox of Churchill's life is that the end seemed so unlikely at the beginning. This Nobel Laureate for Literature was a poor scholar. His military career ended at the substantive rank of lieutenant – those brief months as Lt. Colonel in the Great War are hardly significant – but he is best known to history as a great war leader, the man who took over a baffled nation on the brink of defeat and led it to victory. Any biographer could write a long monograph on the paradoxes of Winston Churchill.

To give another example, consider the glow of esteem that surrounds his 50 year-long political career. Much of this was spent in high office, for Churchill got ahead early, but the enduring admiration for Churchill depends almost entirely on his actions and leadership as

Prime Minister between May 1940 and December 1941 – nineteen months in fifty years. These were the months after Dunkirk and during the Battle of Britain and the Blitz, a time when Great Britain stood alone against the Fascist powers.

Defeat and disaster was staved off by Churchill's courage, his speeches and his example. But for those months of trial and terror it is more than likely that the world at large would have long since forgotten all about a minor British politician called Winston Spencer Churchill. As it is, those months made him, and what he did then will never be forgotten. At that time, Churchill's character made him the ideal man, perhaps at that moment the only man, who could provide what the nation needed.

The true measure of any man is what he stands up for when standing for something is difficult. In 1940-41, Winston Churchill stood for the great abstracts of Western society – democracy, liberty, and justice. That was a lot, and long overdue, but he did so by appealing to the great abiding human virtues of courage, decency, resolve, and endurance. He mustered these human qualities against a great evil that sought to suborn or destroy all those assets if they stood in the way of the State.

Churchill believed, he *really believed,* that good *will* triumph over evil, that men and women are not born to live as slaves and *will* rise against tyranny, that virtue *will* triumph in the end, however long, hard and far-off that end might be. Holding that belief, he roused the nation and led his people to victory over that evil. The world, not only Great Britain, owes Winston Churchill a great debt for what he did in 1940 and 1941.

Churchill was a great man. He had his faults and was not infallible but he was a great man. It has been argued that great men are almost always bad men and there are plenty of examples to make that point. However, if that is true, then that makes Churchill even more remarkable. No one denies he was a great man; in this writer's opinion he was also a good man, a much less common creation in the human experience.

All this being so, his life can be studied with profit, starting here, continuing through any of the larger works given in the bibliography and continuing, if the reader or student is wise, with Churchill's own works. These are extensive, and a pleasure to read, witty, informed, erudite and very entertaining. Indeed, one of the most enjoyable parts of writing this book has been the need to read a great deal of Churchill's own work.

As a taster to that compendium I would urge all readers to obtain a copy of *My Early Life,* Churchill's own biography, which traces his life and times up to 1908. Other works, such as *The World Crisis,* carry his story forward through the First World War and his later work on the Second World War is, in effect, Churchill's life during his time as Prime Minister. In all these books the great man himself comes through, and very entertaining he is.

It remains a regret that in an age where every minor politician now finds it necessary to write memoirs of self-regarding, mind-numbing tedium, Churchill never found the time to carry on his story from *My Early Life* and regale posterity with a full autobiography, told in the same light-hearted and amusing style he used in that lovely book. On the other hand, had he done so, he would have driven so many future studies from the field that the Churchill canon of biographical work would be much smaller than it is.

This then is a brief biography of the life of Winston Spencer Churchill, the great statesman of the 20th century, from his birth in 1874 to his death in 1965. It is the first of a series of brief biographies that will chart the lives of other great leaders in a similar compact fashion, introduce their lives and times to a new generation and serve as an introduction for further study. If this one appeals to you, look for others that will follow shortly.

Robin Neillands
Beckhampton, England
August 2003

Author's Note

I hope that this book – short, direct, non-academic, without a host of footnotes to clog the flow – will direct that growing number of people interested in politics and history towards a further study of the life and times of Winston Spencer Churchill. He lived a colourful life to the full; much can be learned from his example. For those readers interested in the sources used in this book, see my Bibilography.

1. The Early Years

1874 - 1895

'I was a child of the Victorian era,
when the structure of our country seemed firmly set.'

Winston S. Churchill
1932

Winston Spencer Churchill, eldest son of Lord Randolph Churchill and nephew to the eighth Duke of Marlborough, was born at the family seat, Blenheim Palace in Oxfordshire, England, on 30 November, 1874. He died in London ninety-one years later, after a life filled with action, adventure and all the triumphs and pitfalls of high political office. Apart from being a politician and Prime Minister he had also been a Nobel Prize winner, a soldier, a war correspondent, an historian, a writer, a painter, and a bricklayer. He was accorded a State Funeral in London, but after that splendour was buried quietly beside his father in the family plot at Bladon Church on the edge of the Blenheim estate.

The death of Winston Churchill on 24 January, 1965, was mourned in every country. Not only was Churchill a great man, this death marked the end of an era. Since his passing the world has been an emptier and less colourful place; with the death of Churchill the Age of Great Men gave way to a shabbier era, one overfilled with tyrants and political pygmies.

In the long and glorious pantheon of British heroes of history, Winston Churchill ranks supreme. With the possible exception of William Shakespeare, he remains the best-known Englishman to the world at large, somehow surviving the inevitable passing of glory that affects so many once-famous public figures. We shall not see his like again.

But who was he, this dear-departed Englishman? What had he done in that long life to attract such lasting praise and such widespread admiration – and, during his lifetime, be it admitted, not a little criticism, some of it richly deserved? What was his background, how and why did he succeed to such heights, what elements were included in his make-up, and was his rise to fame so unexpected?

To answer those questions is the subject of this book. To find the answers we must go back to a time well before that chill misty morning in 1965 when Winston Spencer Churchill was laid to rest in Bladon churchyard.

When Winston was born, in the height of the Victorian Age, the Churchills were well-established members of the English aristocracy. His father was noted as a rising politician, his grandfather, a previous Duke of Marlborough, had been Lord Lieutenant of Ireland under Mr Disraeli and a great public servant. The family were active in many aspects of public life but the Churchill fame was of quite recent date. Their rise dated back barely 200 years and began with that great general, John Churchill, first Duke of Marlborough, a soldier who had curbed the arrogance of Louis XIV of France and defeated French armies at Malplaquet, Oudenade and Blenheim.

John Churchill was the son of a Cavalier squire, Winston Churchill, who had served Charles I during the Great Rebellion of the 1640's. For his numerous triumphs against the French a generation later, John Churchill had been elevated to a Dukedom and awarded a house and estate, paid for out of public funds and by Royal gifts. Blenheim Palace, a few miles north of Oxford, occupies the lands of the Royal Manor of Woodstock. This was a very suitable spot for a great soldier; another famous warrior, Edward of Woodstock, better known to history as The Black Prince, eldest son of King Edward III and hammer of the Valois, had been born at Woodstock in 1330.

The first Duke barely lived long enough to see his house completed or his line secure. The first Duke and his abrasive and ambitious wife Sarah, long-time confidant of Queen Anne until their most spectacular quarrel, had no male heirs. The Blenheim estate and the title therefore went by special entail to the first Duke's eldest daughter Anne, wife of Clarles Spencer, Earl of Sutherland; the full family name, Spencer Churchill, dates only from 1817.

If well connected, the Spencer Churchills, especially the junior line like Lord Randolph and his family, were not wealthy. The head of the House had barely enough maintain the ducal style, a situation not helped by frequent gambling and chronically excessive expenditure. Nor, after the death of the first Duke, did the family produce another star until Winston Churchill's father, Lord Randolph Henry Spencer Churchill, younger son of the 7th Duke, was born in 1849.

Lord Randolph Churchill, the Member of Parliament for the family constituency of Woodstock, was handsome, dashing, volatile, clever, reckless and extremely ambitious. Lacking money to pursue a political career, he followed the path of many ancient English families – and not a few Dukes of Marlborough – in choosing a rich American heiress as his bride. The bargain in these matches was usually one of mutual satisfaction; the wife provided the money to maintain the family home and keep the husband in his accustomed style and the husband provided a title and entree to upper class society. It was not unknown for the two to fall in love, and this appears to be the case with Lord Randolph and Miss Jennie Jerome.

Miss Jennie Jerome was the younger daughter of Leonard Jerome, a successful American businessman who had made his fortune mining in the Far West – the little town of Jerome in the Yvapai-Apache country of Arizona is still a mining centre. Having made his pile on the far frontier, Mr Jerome departed to make more money on the New York Stock Market, sending his children into society and his daughter to England where she met Lord Randolph. Their courtship was rapid; the couple met at a regatta at the yachting centre of Cowes on the south coast of England in August 1873 and became engaged three days later. She was nineteen and Lord Randolph twenty-four.

The course of true love did not run smoothly; objections to the match came from both sides. The 7th Duke of Marlborough thought that although Miss Jennie was charming, her father was a *parvenu* and that his younger son could do better. Mr Jerome was under no illusions either; while happy to have a young English mi' lord in the family, he was not willing to pay heavily for the privilege. These difficulties were eventually resolved and the couple married in Paris in April 1874 after Mr Jerome had settled the then–substantial sum of £50,000 on his daughter. This was worth around $200,000 at the time but would be worth something in the region of $4,000,000 by present-day values. The capital sum and the income resulting was split equally between husband and wife.

Substantial as this sum was – and it was topped up by a further contribution from the Duke – this produced a combined income of around £3,500 a year, say £150,000 ($220,000) a year at present day (2003) values. This was enough to stave off penury by any standards but not nearly sufficient to maintain the Churchills in their accustomed style – servants, carriages, travel, entertaining, clothes, wine and the annual demands of the London 'Season' with its balls, dinners and entertainments. Chronic money problems were to be one feature of their life which their eldest son would inherit, and largely for the same reason – an ingrained inability to keep expenditure within the bounds of income.

On the other hand, this access of family cash did enable Lord Randolph to fill another ambition and set his feet on the road to power. Members of Parliament were not paid at this time and private means were essential. With these in hand Lord Randolph, who had been elected to the House of Commons in February 1873, began a political career that was brief, brilliant and busy, a life which left little time for his wife and hardly any time at all for his children. The effects of this neglect were to be far reaching.

This, briefly, is the family and the world into which young Winston was born and many of the elements that were to mark his later life were gathered around crib. From his American mother he inherited a life-long love and regard for the United States and its people. From his father came a love of politics and a desire for office and power, and a sense that life was fleeting and should not be wasted. From his ancestors, especially the much-revered first Duke, came physical courage, wide connections, and a deep love of England's history, standards and traditions. Churchill was to build on this inheritance in the years ahead.

Above all, Winston Churchill was an Englishman. In his time it was said, not entirely tongue-in-cheek, that to be born English 'was to start out a winner in the lottery of life.' That may no longer be the case but in the High Victorian Age Britain stood at the peak of her influence and power and a certain amount of satisfaction can hardly be wondered at. The Royal Navy rode the Seven Seas while the British Army guarded an Empire that was usually at peace. That Empire, a source of pride and service to the British people, contained a disparate collection of nations and countries that, if not yet independent, enjoyed a greater measure of justice and freedom than most of them had enjoyed before – or were to enjoy after the Empire ended.

The English – as the British tend to be called outside the nations of their own misty island – were not remotely bashful about their Imperial role. This was the Age of Empire, when every nation that could do so was expanding – the European nations in Africa, the Russians across the steppes into Central Asia, the Americans across the West while establishing hegemony in Latin America – the getting of Empires, in name or in fact, was the current ambition.

The British Empire was simply the largest and most successful of all the colonial empires and, or so the British believed, one much better managed than the rest. It covered about a quarter of the globe and contained about a fifth of the world's population – and all that without adding the influence of the English language and the Anglican Church and Britain's powerful traders. That much of this was now a façade had not yet been noticed; the growing economic power of Germany and the United States, the basic and growing instability in Europe, the failure to invest in higher education and new technology that would undermine Britain and the British Empire, had not yet been noticed or begun to take effect.

On a more local level, Britain had many social problems at home. There was widespread poverty, many towns were little more than industrial slums, there were great divisions between rich and poor, women had yet to get the vote, education was not universally available beyond the primary level and the unions were not yet as powerful or as effective in improving either pay or conditions in the factories as they would soon become. Over all this were the effects of Britain's long-established class system which held many brighter people back from the benefits of education and progressive positions. With all that admitted, Britain at large felt at ease with itself; the people, if poor, were patriotic, there was law in the streets and justice in the courts and a general sense that things were getting better and would continue to do so in the years ahead. Some people, however, were already well ahead in the game of life and among these were the boy Churchill and his parents.

Winston's relations with his parents were never easy. His mother he adored but it seems they were not close. Writing of his childhood he writes of his mother that, 'She shone for me like the Evening Star. I loved her dearly, but at a distance.' It is not too much to say that Lady Jennie neglected her eldest son; not perhaps in material things but in terms of affection and attention. His letters, both from his preparatory school and his public school Harrow, are full of requests for visits and complaints that these requests rarely resulted in his mother's attendence.

His father he clearly loved and admired but their relations were strained; it may be that young Winston was afraid of his father and he certainly tried hard to avoid parental wrath. Winston soon came to feel, or was soon meant to feel, that he was a disappointment to his father. This was so at school and when he entered the Army; try as he would he was never quite able to live up to the demands his father made of him.

For his part, Lord Randolph clearly considered Winston stupid and rarely bothered to conceal this opinion; he supported his son's entry to the Army not because he thought Winston would make a good soldier but because he believed his eldest son lacked the brains to make a career in the law. His mother, while affectionate when they were to hand, much preferred the social round to the cares of her children, Winston and his younger brother Jack. When they went away to school they were 'out of sight and out of mind' and neither parent made much effort to see them.

This unfortunate state of affairs is not uncommon in busy, high-living, socially-active families, but young Winston was sensitive. These feelings, of being kept at a distance from his mother and being a disappointment to his father, left a gap in his life that was filled by his nurse, Mrs Elizabeth Everest, a motherly, good-natured woman from Kent.

'My nurse was my confidante,' wrote Churchill of his child-hood. *'Mrs Everest it was who looked after me and tended all my wants. It was to her I poured out all my many troubles, both now and in my schooldays...She had been born in Chatham and was immensely proud of Kent. No county could compare with Kent, any more than any other country could compare with England...Kent was the place; its capital was Maidstone and around it there grew strawberries, cherries, raspberries and plums. Lovely! I always wanted to live in Kent.'*

If Winston Churchill's childhood sounds privileged but bleak, such a childhood was not unusual at that time and in that society. The then-popular saying among parents of every social class was that 'children should be seen and not heard' but upper-class children were not seen a lot either. A typical aristocratic childhood would be spent in the nursery in the care of a nurse or nanny and the younger servants. The parents would visit the nursery for tea or to say 'Goodnight' to the children but contact in the rest of the day was usually limited. This left a gap in the need for affection which the nurse or nanny filled.

Mrs Everest joined the Churchill household within a few weeks of Winston's birth and stayed for years to look after first Winston and then his younger brother Jack. She remained with the family until Jack left for his public school and remained in close contact with Winston – *'My darling Winny'* as she referred to him in her letters – for the rest of her life. When she died Winston, then a young cavalry officer, was at her bedside.

Winston and Mrs Everest were separated when Winston, now aged 7 and having received some education from a governess, was sent to his preparatory school – *'preparatory schools or 'prep schools' being where the children were prepared for entry into a public school – which in England is an expensive, fee–paying establishment, and not one operated, as in the USA at public expense.'* Winston's first preparatory school, St James at Ascot in Berkshire, appears to have been an upscale version of Dickens *Dotheboys Hall.*

Although possessing the most modern facilities for both education and sport, including that great 19th century innovation, electric light, St James's was noted more for discipline and the severity of its punishments, which were closer to brutality than any academic standards. (Evelyn Waugh, the novelist, was to remark that *'Gaol holds no terrors for anyone who has attended an English public school.'*)

The purpose of St James's was to train boys for entrance to Eton, the top public school in the land. This aim was achieved by long hours of study and liberal applications of the lash; two or three times a month, the whole school was assembled to sit, cowering, while two or three small boys were dragged away and whipped on the buttocks until they bled, their classmates listening to their screams. Churchill was a poor pupil who made little progress under this regime, either in class or on the playing field and suffered accordingly – *'I experienced the fullest application of the secular arm'* as he put it in his memoirs.

After two years of this brutality, after the instigation and insistance of Mrs Everest, Winston was taken away and sent to the kinder climate of a preparatory school in Sussex. There he was much happier and did somewhat better, achieving respectable results in French, history, lots of poetry which he loved and such outdoor pursuits as pony riding and swimming.

Not that the young Winston showed any great signs of academic brilliance, at this time or later – far from it. He survived and he was happy enough but counted each hour and day of term until it was time to return home to Mrs Everest and his massive collection of toy soldiers. This mixture of school and homeward idyll was not to last. For the next step in his education Winston had to go to public school and that required the passage of an entrance exam. The chosen school was Harrow and the exam was said to be difficult – too difficult, it appears, for the 12 year-old Winston Churchill:

'I was unable to answer a single question in the Latin paper. I wrote my name on the top of the page. I wrote down the number of the question '1'. After a while I put a bracket round it thus: (1) After that I could think of nothing either relevant or true. Incidentally, there arrived from nowhere in particular a blot and several smudges. I gazed for two whole hours at this sad spectacle; and then merciful ushers collected my paper and carried it up to the Headmaster's table.'

Nevertheless, in spite of this scanty evidence, the Headmaster of Harrow, Dr Welldon, decided that Winston should be accepted into Harrow and he spent five happy years there. The last three of these were in the Military Class, a class for boys destined for the Army rather than one of the professions or university entrance. Entrance to the law or university required a sound knowledge of Latin and Greek and Churchill never achieved even a modest competence in either subject.

As a result, he stayed in one of the lower forms for much of his time and as a result of that gained a deep grounding in the rhythms and grammer of the English language, which was never to leave him and laid the basis of both his writing and his oratory

Certainly during his schooldays, Winston was not a scholar. He was unable to pass examinations and had little time for those subjects that did not engage his lively imagination. His lack of interest in Latin, Greek, mathematics, or any subject that might pave the path to a worthwhile career and an adequate income was the despair of his tutors and his parents.

On the other hand he shone at history and English, was not unathletic and fond of riding and swimming – and had a remarkable memory, especially for poetry. While at Harrow he once entertained the whole school, and won a prize, by reciting all 1,200 lines of Macaulay's stirring *Lays of Ancient Rome* – on how Horatious held the Bridge, without once referring to the text or making a mistake. Even so, his lack of classical learning put the universities out of his reach and that left only the Services. Lord Randolph agreed that his son should enter the Army – hence Winston's transfer to the Army class.

Winston attributed his father's approval of his choice of career to a rare visit Lord Randoph made to the nursery to inspect Winston's model army, by now amounting to some 1,500 soldiers, which his son had arrayed for battle in all their correct formations. To get into the Army Winston had to pass the exam for Sandhurst, the Royal Military Acadamy, and here again the exams proved the stumbling block. There were five subjects to choose from but mathematics, Latin and English were compulsory and Winston could only hope for a decent result in one of these subjects.

However, his masters at Harrow rallied to the task and at his third try, Winston gained enough marks to earn a cadetship – but in the cavalry, not in the much sought-after infantry arm which was both more highly regarded and somewhat cheaper. Even so, Winston was delighted and wrote enthusiastically to his father to announce this success. His father's response was crushing. His letter recalled every detail of Winston's so far uninspiring educational attainments, deplored the acquiring of a cavalry cadetship, not least on the grounds of cost – *'In the infantry one has to keep a man; in the cavalry a man and a horse as well.'* – and predicted that unless he improved his standards of effort and behaviour his son stood every chance of becoming a wastrel and a social outcast.

Much of this intemperate attack on his son's character and prospects was due to the state of Lord Randolph's health and worries over his declining political career. Lord Randolph had a certain superficial charm and some measure of ability but he was arrogant with a gift for making enemies and choosing the wrong causes at this particular time. He fell out with the Tory Party over fundamental issues like Free Trade and the Irish Question – the independence of Ireland was to bedevil British politics throughout much of the 19th and early 20th century – and was a thorn in the side of successive Prime Ministers.

That said, Lord Randolph had certain skills and in 1886 Lord Salisbury, the newly-elected leader of the Conservative Party, offered him the post of Chancellor of the Exchequer, a high Cabinet post generally regarded as a stepping stone to even higher office. For a few months all went well but in the November of that year, Lord Randolph attempted to overawe his leader with the threat of resignation over some trivial issue. Perhaps regretting the original offer or now knowing his man better, Lord Salisbury accepted this resignation offer with alacrity. Lord Randolph was cast into the political wilderness, never to return.

Nor was this all. The Churchill marriage was also declining. It soon became apparent that Lord Randolph was in poor health, though for a while the cause of his decline, his loss of memory and fits of rage, remained unknown. From 1886 onwards, however, his decline was rapid and he died in 1895 – of *'general paralysis of the insane'* – tertiary syphilis. His last years had been sad and terrible and since he retained his seat in Parliament much of it was in full public view. By 1894 Lord Randoph was clearly ill but he continued to make public appearances and speak at meetings though these speeches were increasingly incoherent – *'He was the chief mourner at his own funeral,'* as Prime Minister Archibald Rosebery remarked in 1896.

Young Winston's feelings at this time can be imagined. He was just 20 when his father died and his father's many mistakes and subsequent fall from power – and the cause of his rapid physical decline thereafter– were soon common knowledge and must have reached Winston's ears. Winston loved his father and had hoped to help him in his political work; the sight of his father's descent into madness, and these constant rejections were deeply wounding. *'If ever I began to show the slightest signs of comradeship,'* wrote Churchill, *'he was immediately offended; and when I once suggested that I might help his private secretary write some of his letters he froze me out completely.'*

There were also problems over money. A cadetship at the Royal Military Academy at Sandhurst, especially a cavalry cadetship, was expensive and funds for his equipment, uniforms, horses and mess bills were hard to find. Lord Randoph's assessment of the need to provide for a horse as well as a man in the cavalry was a considerable underestimate as young Winston later acknowledged; his costs included at least two chargers and one or two hunters and a string of polo ponies, plus a range of uniforms for mess and drill, formal dinners and grand parades. A commission in the Army required a private income that the Churchill finances struggled to provide.

Nor had his father given up on the idea that an infantry cadetship was the best thing for his son. Before Winston entered Sandhurst he had already written to the Commander-in-Chief of the Army, the Queen's cousin, the Duke of Cambridge, requesting help in getting his son commissioned into the 60th Rifles – the King's Royal Rifle Corps – on leaving Sandhurst. Since the Duke of Cambridge was Colonel-in-Chief of that distinguished regiment this was arranged – but on the understanding that Churchill would pass the exam with enough marks for an infantry cadetship. Now that hope was gone and large expenses were added to the family woes.

In spite of these difficulties Churchill went to Sandhurst in the autumn of 1893 and enjoyed every moment of the fifteen–month course. This was a fresh start, a complete break from the trials of his schooldays, entry into a world he enjoyed and excelled at. The Sandhurst course was comprehensive and covered tactics and strategy, fortification, map-making, military law, as well as long hours on the drill parade and in the Riding School.

Winston was already a competent horseman. The Sandhurst riding course was excellent and naturally all the young officers could already ride before joining – there were no motor cars for the young bloods of 1895. In addition his father arranged for further riding lessons with the Royal Horse Guards then billeted in Kensington Barracks and on joining his regiment Winston was put through a further five months training on horsemanship and horse management – taking them all together, he wrote, '*I think I was pretty well trained to sit and manage a horse.*'

Therefore, in spite of his worries Churchill did well and was happy at Sandhurst; he even improved his grades, graduating eighth in a class of 150 in December 1894, a month before his father died in January 1895. Death was to be a constant companion to Churchill thereafter. Reflecting on his class at Sandhurst later he noted that by the mid-1930's only a few – three or four – of his 107 classmates were still alive. The South African War of 1899-1902 accounted for a large proportion and the Great War of 1914-1918 killed almost all the others, and those who survived carried the marks of wounds earned in combat.

In March 1895, two months after the death of his father, Winston Churchil was gazetted into as a 2nd Lieutenant – a cornet – in the 4th Hussars.

The 4th Hussars was a distinguished and fashionable regiment commanded by a remarkable, archetypal, cavalry officer Lt Colonel Brabazon. Colonel Brabazon, an Irish squire, had begun his career in the even more fashionable Grenadier Guards but had been obliged to resign his commission due to a lack of private funds. He then re-enlisted in the ranks of the Grenadiers as a 'gentleman volunteer' and kept up his social connections, which extended to the Prince of Wales, later King Edward VII and membership of clubs in St James and the better country hunts.

Brabazon then served in the Ashanti campaign of 1874 and so distinguished himself that he was restored to commissioned rank and did further service with the 10th Hussars, the Prince of Wales's own regiment, in India until 1893 when he was appointed Colonel of the 4th Hussars. Colonel Brabazon was a character; he had a lisp, actual or affected and chose to ignore the minor problems of life that afflicted lesser mortals. Arriving at Waterloo Station en route for the military base at Aldershot he was informed by a porter that his train had gone. *'Gone?'* said the Colonel. *'Bwing me another.'*

This was the officer who now commanded the young Lt Winston Churchill, and this was a fortunate conjunction, for few other commanding officers would have tolerated this young officer, with his strong desire for action and his scant regard for regimental duties. Within weeks of joining the 4th Hussars young Churchill was on the lookout for action and casting eyes on the only source available, a rebellion in the Spanish colony, Cuba.

Before anything could be arranged Winston had to address certain problems following the death of his father. His parents had lived well and entertained lavishly but were by no means rich, and when his father's estate had been through probate it was discovered that Lord Randoph's assets were almost completely eliminated by his debts. These debts were duly paid and the Churchills, mother and two sons, were left on the entail from her marriage settlement which allowed for comfort and security but left little over for extravagance; Lady Jennie allowed her son £500 a year in quarterly instalments. With that and his pay he must survive.

His salary was just £150 ($220)a year, around 70 pence a day, but the regiment were destined for service in India where allowances and a lower cost of living would increase the value of that sum to around £300 ($450) – still a long way short of the sums an officer needed to pay his way in the Army.

And finally before closing this chapter in his life, there was another sadness for young Winston Churchill; in 1896 Mrs Everest died. Mrs Everest had looked after both the Churchill boys and was now very ill with peritionitis – then fatal – her one desire was to see her boys. Churchill spent two days at her bedside and writing in his memoirs long after her death remembered her as ' *the dearest and most intimate friend during the whole of the twenty years I had lived.*' Churchill never forgot Mrs Everest and later on in his political career, *thinking of the fate of other poor old women, he was glad to take a hand in the structure of a pensions scheme which is expecially a help to them.*'

The death of his father and his old nurse broke Churchill's remaining ties with his youth. On the whole, in spite of his academic failures, it had not been a bad education; he had known grief and hardship as well as luxury and learned that the poor had value as much as the rich. He had the self-confidence common to his class and a range of useful connections but no ties to bind him. His mother remained, a source of affection and a constant support, but from now on Winston Spencer Churchill was on his own in the world. What his future would become, and where it would lead, was entirely up to him.

2. A First Taste of Action

1895 -1897

'Twenty to twenty–five! Those are the years!
You cannot hurt the world or even seriously distress her.
She was made to be wooed and won by youth.'

Winston S. Churchill

When Winston Churchill joined his regiment in the Spring of 1895, the 4th Hussars were on garrison duty in Aldershot, the home of the British Army, forty miles south of London. It was then the custom in the British Army that a new officer, however high his social status in civilian life, should spend the first six months in the ranks. During this time he would take the same training course followed by the other recruits and discover what they had been taught – though the young officer was naturally expected to try harder and do perceptibly better than the twenty or so rankers who made up the balance of the squad. Only in this way could a young officer really appreciate what the men knew; only by sharing their experiences could a subaltern learn how important it is to lead rather than drive – and that the basis of command is a willingness to obey.

Churchill seems to have enjoyed this time in training; even the rigours of yet another riding course with all its bumps and spills did not deter him, but he was already looking around for a chance to find adventure and make a name for himself. At any other time it should have been easy to find action somewhere on the widely-spread frontiers of the British Empire, but in 1895 the British Empire was at peace. That peace would soon be broken, but Churchill had to cast about for action in the meantime.

This being so, Churchill duly looked around, pulled a few strings and applied to his Commanding Officer for leave to visit the island of Cuba – if he could not be sent there officially as an Army observer – where the settlers were in armed revolt against their Spanish rulers. The life of a British Army officer in those distant days was not unduly taxing; it consisted of seven months of training during the summer months and five months of leave – furlough – of which up to three months could be taken at any one time.

This allowed ample time for recreation but a young officer was supposed to devote his leisure to manly exercises – hunting, shooting, mountain climbing, anything with an element of risk. Any young man caught in the equally hazardous pastime of chasing the ladies – 'poodlefaking' in the jargon of the time – could find his leave curtailed and his promotion prospects dim.

Thanks to Colonel Brabazon, Churchill had no difficulty in obtaining permission to visit Cuba. Hving written to an old friend of his father, the British Ambassador in Madrid, for the necessary permissions, in November 1895 Churchill and another 4th Hussars subaltern, Reginald Barnes, set out for Cuba via New York and were made warmly welcome on arrival in Cuba by the Spanish commander in the campaign against the insurgents, Marshal Martinez Campos.

Marshal Campos commanded some 80,000 regular Spanish soldiers, apparently more than enough to end the rebellion – but his campaign was not prospering. The rebels refused to stand and fight but chipped away steadily at the Regulars. This guerrilla fighting caused a steady stream of casualties among Campos's men as the Spanish columns advanced over plain and mountain and attempted, without much success, to drive the rebels into the open. It was Churchill's first taste of irregular warfare, the kind of fighting with which he would soon be all too familiar, and one which thereafter always attracted his close attention.

This was his first taste of real soldiering, campaigning on horseback with loaded weapons against an active enemy. The rebels were first encountered on 30 November, 1895 – Churchill's 21st birthday – when a small party appeared and opened fire on the Spanish column, emptying a few saddles and killing a horse. On the following day there was more firing from the surrounding jungle and sporadic fighting continued for the next few days as the column proceeded at a somewhat leisurely pace across the mountains. Churchill records that although not many men were hit, rebel bullets frequently raked the entire length of the column and when the enemy did elect to stand and fight, several men and more horses were killed.

This foray was of short duration but Churchill was able get his first experience of being under rifle fire – an experience which he always found exciting if not even actually enjoyable; during the Second World War he declared to a group of US generals that, *'Nothing is so exhilarating as to be shot at without effect.'* Being under fire for the first time is always a memorable experience and a useful one; Churchill determined to experience this again – and if next time he could get a medal in the process, so much the better.

On his way home following this brief visit to Cuba, Churchill made a short stop in New York, the first of many visits to the United States. On this occasion he was made very welcome in the home of one of his mother's former admirers, Bourke Cochran, a Republican politician, a member of the House of Representatives, a candidate in the 1892 Presidential election – and a very rich man. Cochran's lavish hospitality, the vibrancy of New York life, and this short experience of American life made a great and lasting impression on Churchill. *'This is a very great country,'* he wrote to his brother Jack and he never wavered from that early opinion.

This first visit to the United States may also have provided Churchill with a long-lasting asset. In 1955 Churchill was asked by the American politician and statesman Adlai Stevenson, where he had learned his famous oratorical style? Much to Stevenson's surprise, Chuchill replied, *'Here in America, from Bourke Cochran, who taught me how to use the human voice, how to play on the vocal cords as on an organ.'* This anecdote may well be correct; Churchill did not have a clear speaking voice, certainly in his early years in politics and was always afflicted with a slight lisp. His great speeches are exercises in the use of vocal tones to portray various emotions – defiance, resolution, pity – and these tones came to have as much impact as the words themselves. Hearing one of Churchill's speeches is a far more powerful experience than merely reading one.

Churchill also practised his speeches, much as an opera singer learns and practises an *aria,* matching words to tones and both words and tones to gestures, the whole combining to make a strong impression on the listener; even many of his apparently off-the-cuff remarks were pre-planned and carefully rehearsed – though he could and did summon up the cutting comment or the quick riposte when the opportunity arose.

A popular anecdote illustrating the latter arose when he was first seeking election to Parliament in 1900. Churchill approached a voter in the street asking for his support in the coming election. *' Vote for you?'* said the man, *' I'd rather vote for the Devil.'*

'I quite understand,' said Churchill, *' but since that person is not running this time, perhaps I could count on your support?'*

Churchill was back with his regiment by the beginning of 1896 and took part in all the necessary preparations before sailing for India at the end of the summer, arriving in Bombay in October 1896. The British Empire was at its zenith, a source of pride and inspiration to the British people, and India was the jewel of all its far-flung territories. Churchill was, and remained, an unrepentant imperialist. He saw the stability of the Empire and the honesty of its servants as a force for good in the world, and it is one of the tragedies of his life that the Empire he was born into and devoted a lifetime's service had all but disappeared by the time of his death – although at least he was spared the bitter knowledge of what happened in so many former colonies in the decades after the British left.

The core of the British Empire, the jewel in the Imperial Crown, was India. Not all of India was directly under British control – about a third of the country was ruled by the Indian Princes, rajahs, maharajahs and nawabs who ruled their ancestral territories under the broad guidance and light control of the Viceroy in Delhi. The rest of India was under British control with the Viceroy in his alternative role of Governor-General, who was also responsible for the defence of the turbulent Frontier.

This was the *Raj,* British India, a vast territory guarded and controlled, but not oppressed by two distinct forces, the Indian Army which had Indian troops and British officers, and the British Army in India which was entirely British. The British Army in India was not large – it mustered some 50,000 men in the entire sub–continent, which had a population of around 400 million. As a rule, the Indian Army guarded the frontiers and the more phlegmatic British troops handled internal security and supressed riots which came from the constant threat of civil disturbance between the mutually hostile Hindu and Muslim communities.

British rule in India was firm but benign. As a result there was usually very little for the soldiery to do. For the men in the ranks, deprived of their families, life was tedious, but for the officers, with plenty of leave, hosts of servants, and many opportunities for sport, especially hunting and shooting – *shikar* – life could be extremely pleasant. This was the life that Winston Churchill entered into at the end of 1896 and he found it not at all to his taste.

The basic problem was boredom, ambition, and a lack of funds. Churchill always had a very low boredom threshold and no amount of shooting, hunting, and polo, however enjoyable, could make up for a lack of action. Like his fellow officers in the cavalry base at Bangalore, Churchill played polo every day and became a first-class player but sport was not enough to keep him entertained. He was ambitious and felt the need to make a name for himself quickly. For that he needed action and in this Churchill was following the path of other ambitious officers, not least the current Commander-in-Chief of the British Army, Lord Wolseley, who had declared at the start of his long and distinguished career that, *'The way for a man to get on in the Army was to try and get himself killed as often as possible.'*

The problem for Churchill was that the Empire was quiet. Between the end of the Napoleonic Wars in 1815 and the start of the First World War – the Great War – in 1914, Great Britain fought seventeen wars in or around the fringes of the Empire. All was quiet for Churchill until 1897, while on leave in England, Churchill heard that a punitive expedition, a Field Force of three Brigades, was to be mounted in India against the hostile Pathan tribes in the Malakand who had been raiding into British India.

Moreover, this expedition was to be commanded by General Sir Bindon Blood, who was known to Churchill and had promised that should he ever get command of such an expedition, Churchill could go along. A cable was promptly despatched to Sir Bindon, reminding him of this promise and the reply, if not effusive, *'Very Difficult. No Vacancies. Come as a correspondent; will try to fit you in.'* BB. This brief missive was enough to send Churchill racing for the Calais boat train.

Getting a taste of frontier action was not Churchill's only objective. He also needed to make some money and intended to finance the trip, improve his bank balance, and establish his journalistic credentials by writing about the Malakand Field Force for the British newspapers. Thanks to the influence of Lady Jennie this latter aim was fairly successful; he was commissioned to write columns for the *Daily Telegraph* at the rate of £5 a column – say £150 at present-day rates – and at a smaller rate for an Indian newspaper, the *Pioneer*. So began a parallel career in freelance journalism that would keep Churchill afloat financially in many of the lean years ahead.

Lacking any writing or journalistic credentials, getting paid commissions from newspaper editors and permission to act as military correspondent on punitive expedition from his military superiors was not easy. but Churchill had certain advantages. He was the son of a Lord and the nephew of a Duke and his family had long-standing political and military connections.

That apart, Churchill never lacked self–confidence. He was always quick to push himself forward and, in the best traditions of politics and journalism, never let his total ignorance of any particular situation prevent him expressing an opinion. At this time he was, to be blunt, a bumptious and opinionated young man and this aspect of his character did not go down too well with either his regimental colleagues or the senior officers. Even so, when an anxious Churchill arrived at Bangalore and asked for permission to join the Field Force, his Colonel approved of this zest for combat and gave the necessary approval. Churchill joined the Malakand Field at the Nowshera rail head, close to the Frontier at the end of August 1897 – after a 2,000 mile journey from Bangalore that took five full days by rail. From here it was another 40 miles across the plains to the foot of the Malakand Pass to find Sir Bindon and his Staff camped at the summit.

The first task was to subdue the local tribe, the Bunerwals, and that took another five days. The Bunerwals were a notorious tribe and one point higher in the pass was littered with the bones of British soldiers and Burnerwals killed in previous fighting around the Malakand. Churchill took no part in this early fighting and the only lesson learned while waiting was the merits of a Scotch and soda, thus acquiring a taste for Scotch whisky that never left him. He also acquired two ponies and a groom and some campaign equipment, much of the latter being picked from the kit of officers already killed in the first skirmishes.

The British Army had held the summit of the Malakand Pass for several years and so kept open the road from the plains to the Chitral valley. This infidel presence irritated the local tribesmen and now they were in revolt, had already slaughtered a number of the civilian population – all Indian – and attacked the British garrison at the Chakdara Fort, which had held out until relieved. The aim now was to crush this revolt and discourage further incursions by marching into the mountains, through the Dir and Bajaur valleys and so back to the plains. This would involve marching through the territory of another warlike Pathan tribe, the Mamund, but as soon as Sir Bindon Blood returned from his forays against the Bunarwals, the campaign began.

From Churchill's account in *My Early Life*, the Malakand Expedition was regarded by the British and the Pathans as a kind of lethal game – and one in which the Political Officers, the British officials charged with maintaining peace on the Frontier – were seen as biased referees, who interfered to call off the fight just as it got interesting. '*On the other side*' wrote Churchill '*we had the very strong spirit of the 'die-hards' and the 'young bloods' of the enemy. We wanted to shoot at them and they wanted to shoot at us.*'

The dangers in this kind of campaign should not be underestimated from these light-hearted comments; Frontier warfare was extremely dangerous. The Pathans took no prisoners. Any soldier wounded and left behind would be cut to pieces – so it was a point of honour that no one was ever left behind.

The North West Frontier can be imagined as not unlike the American West in the period immediately after the Civil War though the scenery is, if anything even more spectacular and unrelieved by green valleys or wide plains. Instead great snowtipped mountains rear up on every side, every valley contains a tribe, every village is a fortified camp and every house a redoubt. The inhabitants of this wild country are the Pathans – ferocious warriors, given to the vendetta and delighting in combat – especially against the infidel white soldiers from the soft plains of India.

Churchill got his first taste of this kind of fighting on the first day. After a long march his brigade went into bivouac and immediately came under accurate sniper fire from the surrounding slopes. No great harm was done but fires had to be put out, dinner eaten in the dark, and picquets 'stood-to' all night, on the alert for infiltration and rifle thieves.

At daylight, the resistance to their advance increased as the hills around were occupied by tribesmen who poured a heavy fire into the troops and animals mustered in the valley below. There were now hundreds of tribesmen around the column and some 40 men and a number of horses and pack animals were killed or wounded in the first day of fighting. To beat these opponents off, Sir Bindon ordered General Jefferys, commanding the 2nd Brigade, to enter the Mahmoud valley and teach the locals a lesson; Sir Bindon also agreed that Churchill could go on this mission.

On September 16, Jefferys' force entered the Mahmoud Valley, Churchill riding with a party of 15 scouts from the Bengal Lancers. The enemy were soon encountered and Churchill's party dismounted and opened fire with their carbines at a distance of around 700 yards. The Pathans replied with a heavy volume of fire, but the range was long and no great damage was done in the next hour while the infantry of the 35th Sikhs came up and deployed for the attack.

Churchill then handed his pony to a bearer and joined the infantry as they trudged up the slope, the enemy fire dying away as the advance continued. After about an hour Churchill stopped for a rest and noted with not particular alarm that his party had shrunk somewhat; instead of a full battalion he seemed to be with only about 90 men, including five British officers who had somehow got ahead of all the other troops and were at the head of the valley.

Recalling his recent Sandhurst lessons on tactics, it occurred to Churchill that this party might have gone too far, but the advance continued until they entered a small village which appeared deserted. Churchill and an infantry section of eight Sikhs were put out as a cordon while the rest of the village was searched; then a captain arrived and ordered a withdrawal.

Withdrawing was never easy on the Frontier. That was the time that the watching tribesmen – who had fallen back before the advance – usually chose to put in a counter-attack and so it was here. As the

Sikhs fell back, section by section and platoon by platoon 'the whole mountainside sprang to life. Swords flashed and bright flags waved here and there. A dozen white smoke puffs broke from the rugged face in front of us.'

Hundreds of tribesmen were now rushing upon them, rushing from rock to rock, firing as they came, waving swords, yelling war cries, attempting to drive the Sikh battalion back in confusion and cut off small parties for destruction. Churchill borrowed a single-shot Martini-Henry rifle from a sepoy and began to return this fire while the sepoy handed him cartridges. This went on for about five minutes until the battalion adjutant appeared and ordered Churchill and his section to fall back while the rest of the Company gave covering fire – as they got up to move a volley killed two Sikhs and wounded four more, including the British adjutant – and at this moment the enemy charged.

There was a violent battle on the slope as the Sikhs grabbed their wounded and attempted to fight back and fall back. Fire was now being poured upon them but it was a point of honour not to leave the wounded. Then the four men carrying the Adjutant were charged by a group of Pathans, and they dropped him and the first Pathan slashed him to death with a sword. Churchill relates that 'I forgot everything else at this moment except a desire to kill this man'.

Churchill drew his sabre and charged back up the slope but as more Pathans came charging forward, he pulled out his revolver and opened fire, hitting his man after two shots. Churchill then realised he was quite alone and ran back though a hail of bullets to regain his company and fall back with them to the bottom of the hill, where the 35th Sikhs reassembled as hundreds of Pathans formed a half moon around their flanks and raked them with fire. The Colonel of the Sikhs decided to make a stand here – one which was taking on all the features of a last stand – and ordered Churchill to go back and bring up the supporting battalion from The Buffs.

Churchill requested the order in writing and was right to do so. Had the Sikhs been overwhelmed while he was absent, it might have been said later that he had abandoned them, but as the Colonel wrote our the order and the battalion began to fire volleys into the surrounding tribesmen, the first files of the Buffs came scrambling up the hill towards them. The Sikhs then went back up the hill to recover the body of the Adjutant and about 20 officers and men of the Company who had fallen in the action.

The campaign in the Mahmoud Valley continued for another two weeks. There was fighting every day and every day about 20 men were killed or wounded but Sir Bindon Blood ordered General Jefferys to keep his brigade in the valley until all resistance had ceased and the valley itself was a wasteland. There was fighting for every hilltop and village but in the end this mission was accomplished. '*Whether it was worth it I cannot tell*', says Churchill, '*at the end of a fortnight the valley was a desert, and honour was satisfied.*'

During the later stages of this campaign Churchill was attached to the 31st Punjab Infantry which only had four white officers left from the 32 it had started out with. Churchill was a cavalier officer and spoke not a word of Punjabi but he commanded his company successfully in several skirmishes while continuing to send a stream of dispatches to the *Daily Telegraph*.

Meanwhile the Pathan revolt was spreading. Churchill attributes this to the success the Pathans had had against the 35th Sikhs in the Mahmoud Valley, a success that had been widely reported in the Pathan villages. Whatever the reason, the powerful Afridi tribe from Tirah was now in the field and the Governor General therefore decided that it was necessary to send another expedition to Tirah as the Malakand expedition marched home.

Being already in the field and hardened by battle, Churchill thought that his application for the Tirah campaign was only a formality, but it was not to be. Sir Bindon Blood was to stay on the Malakand while the Tirah Force would be commanded by an officer unknown to Churchill, Sir William Lockhart. Churchill did have one contact, Colonel Ian Hamilton, whom he had met on a musketry course and now commanded one of the Tirah brigades, but Colonel

Hamilton was injured in a riding accident and had to withdrew from the Expedition.

The Tirah Expedition would be a much larger affair, involving six brigades instead of the three deployed in the Malakand and Churchill was very anxious to be included – cabling his mother to pull every string as before – but his Colonel and his brother officers decided that Lt Churchill had seen more than his fair share of action and should return to the regiment in Bangalore. This time no amount of pleading or string pulling made any difference.

Not long after his return to Bangalore Churchill took ten days local leave over Christmas and employed it in making the seven-day round trip to Calcutta, intending to ask the Viceroy, Lord Elgin, to intercede with the Commander–in–Chief, India, General Sir George White, and persuade him to order Sir William Lockhart to find a place for Lt Churchill. This proposal met with a chilly reception in every quarter. Churchill was welcomed and royally entertained to dinner, parties, and polo but he was also made very well aware that any mention of the Tirah Expedition and his inclusion in it was not one that would attract attention, let alone favour. Somewhat downcast, he returned to his regiment.

During this time, in the winter of 1896 both before and after the Malakand expedition, Churchill had decided to improve on his somewhat sketchy education and wrote to his mother asking her to send out a stream of classic works. He was always an autodidact and never more so than now as he ploughed steadily though the classical and historical works of Gibbon – *The Decline and Fall of the Roman Empire* and Macaulay's *History of England* as well as Darwin's *Origin of Species,* Adam Smith's *Wealth of Nations*, Plato's *Republic* and, interestingly, the complete Parliamentary Register for the last twenty years, which gave a detailed account of every debate in the House of Commons. The works consulted included books on American history including the politics and strategy of the US Civil War. Now that these subjects had some relevance to his future and the process of study interested him, he had no difficulty getting to grips with their contents – the scholar and historian in Churchill was starting to emerge.

Churchill records that he spent four or five hours a day at this sturdy over a period of months; because he approached this study with a hungry mind he absorbed these texts steadily and profitably, beginning to envy those younger men who had moved on smoothly from their public schools to university and enjoyed such a profitable occupation in their early years, unworried by regimental duties or the need to make a living. Churchill was to read steadily for the rest of his life but never as omnivourously as over the next two years when, in effect, he gave himself a classical education.

One result of all this study was a change, or at least a certain shift, in Churchill's political opinions and the emergence of political ambition. Born into a Tory family, educated among Tories and now in daily contact with diehard Tories in the regimental mess his political adherence had always been to the Conservative values common to his class. Now he began to find some merit in the Liberal-Whig tradition, even declaring that were it not for the issue of Home Rule for Ireland, to which he was firmly opposed, he would seek election to a Liberal seat. Failing that he took up the position of a Tory Democrat, someone who judges an issue on its merits and not by the Party line.

It seems unlikely that Winston Churchill ever had the makings of a good regimental officer. The routine of regimental life was not for him and the rejection of all his efforts to join the Tirah Expedition indicated that he would not be allowed to put his private wishes for action before the daily constraints of regimental duty. He actually spent very little time with his regiment and was thinking of resigning his commission and either entering politics or going to university long before his time in India was over. Churchill actually spent less than two years with the 4th Hussars and in that time, though based in Bangalore, he fitted in two Home Leaves, three local leaves, various tours with the regimental polo team, and a journalistic assignment to the North West Frontier to cover the activities of the Malakand Field Force.

The Malakand expedition, brief as it was – the entire affair lasted just six weeks and Churchill was back at the 4th Hussar cantonment in Bangalore by the middle of October – provided the basis for the first of Churchill's many books. *The Story of the Malakand Field Force,* an 85,000 word manuscript, was finished and posted to his mother by the end of the year. Lady Jennie had plenty of connections and the book was published by Longmans in May 1898, attracting a gratifying number of favourable reviews and the useful advance against royalties of some £600 ($900) – worth around $50,000 in today's dollars, a substantial advance for a new author.

That apart, his despatches in the *Daily Telegraph*, although written under the byline of *A Young Officer,* for serving officers were not allowed to write for the Press without official permission, had also been well received, a success that promised further profitable employment. This time in India and the Malakand expedition in particular marks several steps in Churchill's development.

He had displayed the finest of all gifts – personal courage. Without courage nothing is possible. He had commanded troops under fire in the field against a determined and ruthless enemy. He had turned his hand to journalism with success and written his first book with even greater success. He had done all his without becoming arrogant or getting his head turned. Churchill had always had plenty of self-confidence, but a lively sense of humour prevented this useful asset exceeding acceptable limits and toppling over into bombast and conceit.

Churchill had clearly developed a taste for writing and showed considerable ability and pleasure in the process. While his Malakand book was making its way through the publishing process, he was also attempting his one and only novel, *Savrola,* a tedious work, now long out of print and best ignored by Churchill devotees; in later life Churchill begged his friends not to read it. There was also the other benefit of this new-found skill – money.

Like any young officer without substantial private means, even in India Churchill was chronically hard up. He noted with pleasure that this one book had in the space of a few weeks earned him more money than he would have earned in two years as an Army subaltern. The thought that authorship and journalism might be the way to sustain himself in civilian life and fund his career in politics crossed his mind at this time but there was a snag with leaving the Army and chancing his all on a freelance career.

The Imperial peace of recent years was coming to an end. There was the prospect of action in half a dozen countries, most notably in South Africa and Egypt and the way to get to any coming conflict, find action and adventure and the copy for more books and articles seemed to lie with the continuation of his military career.

Indeed, the writing and publication of his current work was interrupted by yet another military venture. The Army was on the march again in Africa and Churchill was anxious to work his way as officer and correspondent onto the next imperial venture: General Sir Herbert Kitchener's expedition to the Sudan in 1898-99, a hard and bitter campaign against the Dervishes that culminated in the battle of Omdurman.

3. Churchill at the Charge

1898

'Out of my way, you drunken swabs!'

Morning greeting by General Herbert Kitchener
to a group of war correspondents, the Sudan, 1898

To trace the origins of Britain's last colonial venture in the
Victorian era, General Sir Herbert Kitchener's expedition up the Nile
to Khartoum and Omdurman in 1897-98, one must go back to the
opening of the Suez Canal in 1869 and the British occupation of Egypt
in 1882. So began the British involvement with the affairs of Egypt and
the Sudan – later the Anglo-Egyptian Sudan – which was to last until
the end of the British Empire in the 1950's.

The Suez Canal was constructed as a co-operative venture between
the French and the Egyptians. The snag for Britain was that when
completed it offered a short sea route to the Far East and, rather more
to the point in British eyes, a quick means of reaching India. This,
clearly, was a great boost to peacetime trade but should there be a war
with, say, the French and the French had possession of the Suez Canal,

45

they could quickly send forces to the East while British troopships were still ploughing the roundabout route via the Cape of Good Hope.

This strategic factor alone made possession or at least control of the Suez Canal vital to British interests. When the Khedive of Egypt defaulted on his massive debts in 1882, Britain as one of the major creditors proceeded to take over the country and reorganise its economy. The British had purchased the Khedive's interest in the Canal in 1875 for the bargain sum of £4 million (say $16 million dollars). Benjamin Disraeli, the Prime Minister, borrowed the money from the Rothschild family to avoid waiting for Parliamentary approval.

It was this strategic need to control the Suez Canal and not any particular interest in Egypt's financial predicament that sent British troops to seize Egyptian territory and civil servants to sort out the Egyptian economy. There was, however, a further problem with this Egyptian involvement, one that Britain could well have done without. With control of Egypt came responsibility for the affairs of the Sudan.

Like Egypt, the Sudan was a possession of the declining Ottoman Empire. Egypt, if corrupt and insolvent, had at least the outlines of a civilized administration by the end of the 19th century. The Sudan, on the other hand, was arid, barren, remote, the largest country in Africa, and the next best thing to a hell-on-earth. The main occupation of the Sudan was the slave trade and the Arab or Egyptian inhabitants of the Sudan were either slave traders or in some way connected with the slave trade. The only other occupation was trading in the far less profitable gum-arabic, a product of the acacia tree used to make ink. Basically, in 1882, the British Empire, which had abolished slavery in 1803 and spent most of the previous decades suppressing it, suddenly found itself back with the slave trade.

From the Sudan capital, Khartoum, slave traders raided south into Central Africa along the axis of the Nile, scouring what is now Uganda for slaves, attacking and despoiling the native villages and African tribes. Those captured would be brought to the Sudan, the women raped *en route* and the men kept either for hard labour in the cotton fields or castrated at the port of Suakin from which the survivors of this brutality would be shipped across the Red Sea and sold to the markets and harems of Arabia.

The Egyptian Government had either tolerated or encouraged this trade; many slaves were sent north to work in the cotton fields of Egypt but the British had abolished slave trading in the 1820's and taken a major role in the abolition of slavery wherever found. During the 19th century the Royal Navy had been busily engaged in stemming the slave trade, explorers like Livingstone and the London based Anti-Slavery Society kept the British public fully aware of the horrors of the African slave trade. As a result the British arrived in Egypt fully intending to wipe out the slave trade in the Sudan.

This was to prove difficult. Even today, less then 50 years after Britain gave up the Sudan in the 1950s, there is still a substantial slave trade in the Sudan. In the 1880s Britain's main instrument in attacking the Sudanese slave trade was an officer in the Royal Engineers, Colonel Charles Gordon. Their main obstacle was a native mystic and chieftain, the *Mahdi* – 'The Expected One' – who had come to power in the Sudan in 1881. The Mahdi was not at all concerned about the slave trade; his aim was to free the Sudan from Egyptian control and direct all Muslims back to the true path – which the Mahdi would define.

The first attempt to destroy the power of the Mahdi and his followers, the Dervishes, was made in 1883 by an Egyptian army commanded by a British officer, Hicks Pasha. The Dervishes lured this army deep into the waterless desert south of Khartoum and slaughtered Hicks Pasha and his army to the last man, acquiring in the process thousands of modern rifles and a quantity of field artillery. This disaster required an immediate and resolute response from London but the current Prime Minister, Mr Gladstone, had no intention of getting involved in the Sudan, even declaring that the British Empire was already far too big and far too costly. The British therefore decided to leave the Mahdi and his forces in control of the Sudan, but evacuate all the Egyptian and Europeans in Khartoum to safety. The man sent to effect this evacuation was Charles Gordon.

The character and reputation of Major-General Gordon falls outside the boundaries of this book (for a full account of Gordon and the Sudan campaign see *The Dervish Wars: Gordon and Kitchener in the Sudan* by Robin H. Neillands, 1996). Suffice to say that Charles Gordon was a hero to the British public and a great trial to his superiors, military and political. Matters were not helped by confusion over his orders.

Charles Gordon was sent to Khartoum with two sets of orders. The Prime Minister in London told him to make a report on the situation in Khartoum for the British Government's consideration. The British Resident in Cairo, Sir Evelyn Baring, did not need another report; he ordered Gordon to get up to Khartoum and evacuate the civilians and the Egyptian garrison forthwith.

Unfortunately for all concerned, Charles Gordon was not noted for his obedience to orders, and having arrived in Khartoum he elected for a third course of action. He decided to stay there and fight it out with the Mahdi and the subsequent siege of Khartoum lasted many months, from the summer of 1884 to the winter of 1885.

During that time the image of this gallant British officer and Christian gentleman, holding a lonely outpost in the desert while surrounded by hordes of howling Muslim savages, attracted the attention of the world. It also so electrified Queen Victoria and the British public that eventually – in the gritted teeth of opposition from Mr Gladstone – an expedition was mounted to rescue Gordon from disaster.

This expedition, commanded by General Sir Garnet Wolseley, set out from Cairo in October 1884. After a nightmare passage up the Nile in the face of stiff opposition from the Dervishes – and several costly battles – the Gordon Relief Expedition arrived at Khartoum on 28 January, 1885, two days after the Dervishes had overwhelmed the defences of Khartoum, massacred the garrison, and cut off General Gordon's head.

There was a considerable outcry in Britain and the fall of Khartoum swiftly led to the fall of Gladstone's Government. The new British Government then wisely decided to leave the Dervishes and the Sudan alone. So it remained for another eleven years, until 1896, when it was thought necessary to mount an expedition into the Sudan to help the Italian conquest of Abyssinia, now Ethiopia, after the Abyssinian warriors had not only defeated the Italian Army at Adowa but also castrated all their Italian prisoners.

Nor was this all; the French were on the move and had despatched Captain Phillipe Marchand on an expedition west-to-east across Africa, intending to occupy territory on the Upper Nile. This French project, if successful, would block Britain's long-held intention of holding territory all the way from Cairo to the Cape and building a railway to link the Mediterranean with the South Atlantic. All in all, the Sudan had to be reoccupied and an expedition was mounted to carry out that intention. This was the expedition commanded by General Sir Herbert Kitchener, the one Churchill was desperate to join – and General Kitchener was equally determined to keep him out of.

This was not due to any particular animosity between Kitchener and Churchill. It is unlikely that the great Kitchener, currently 'Sirdar' (Commander-in-Chief) of the Egyptian Army, had heard much about a 23-year old cavalry cornet called Winston Churchill, though anything he had heard would not have been to Churchill's credit. In higher military circles Winston was currently regarded as a 'pot hunter,' always chasing glory at the cost of his regimental duties. These duties and Churchill's regiment were in India, where this young officer had already had more than his share of action; he should stay there and earn his pay and give others a chance in the Sudan.

Kitchener's real objection was to Winston's other incarnation as a member of that new breed of military parasite, the war correspondent, that gang of inquisitive, intrusive, opinionated journalists, amateur or professional, who hung about Kitchener's tent day and night and were brusquely brushed aside every morning. Relations between Kitchener and the Press were never good and Churchill, an Army officer clutching a number of newspaper commissions and anxious for accreditation, was just the sort of man Kitchener loathed.

A closer investigation of Churchill's requests did nothing to soften the Sirdar's attitude. He also came to regard Churchill as a jumped-up, medal-hunting young jackanapes; all too eager to use his aristocratic connections to gain a place that better and more experienced soldiers aspired to. It therefore took Winston most of 1897 and well into the early months of 1898 to get permission to go to the Middle East and join the Sudan expedition, which was still making its slow and painful way up the Nile cataracts. Churchill's need to join rose with every rejection, for British public attention were now fixed on the Nile; the death of Gordon eleven years before had not been forgotten and the Nile campaign was one every soldier and journalist wanted to take part in.

Getting up 1,000 miles of rocky, turbulent river from the Nile Delta to Khartoum could not be managed in a single season. In the event it took the best part of three years, all in the face of Dervish opposition – not to mention disease, a great number of biting insects, and a chronic shortage of water. The climate and the Dervishes took a steady toll of the British, Egyptian, and Sudanese soldiers but their relentless advance continued. Their efforts culminated in a battle astride one of the Nile tributaries, the Atbara River, on 5 April, 1898, an encounter which gave General Kitchener a narrow victory. The coming campaign season – a final thrust up to Khartoum – was clearly going to be decisive and Churchill was desperate to be in at the kill.

Fortunately, his participation in the Malakand Expedition had entitled Churchill to yet another spot of home leave. He duly sailed for the UK in the spring of 1898, half-hoping that Kitchener would relent and let him leave the ship in Port Said and head south along the Nile. There was no response in Egypt to his frequent pleas, so Churchill sailed on to London, though he left his Indian servant behind in Cairo, with all his expedition equipment, pending his anticipated return.

Once in London, enlisting the support of Lady Jennie, Churchill lost no time in pulling every string available. By now he had a dual intention, not simply to get down the Nile to Khartoum but also to advance his other growing ambition, a political career. To this latter end he spoke at a Tory Party meeting in Bradford, a Yorkshire mill town, giving a speech on the Malakand Field Force and some political opinions, both of which attracted a gratifying amount of favourable Press comment.

Other matters, not least his financial affairs, were less promising, and Churchill was obliged to reduce the capital amount funding his current income in order to pass the massive capital sum of £14,000 ($56,000 then – but say $600,000 in modern money) over to his improvident mother. This was not easy to do, but filial devotion triumphed over childhood neglect and this large sum was duly paid over – and as quickly spent. The *quid pro quo* was that Lady Randolph would employ her not inconsiderable charms and connections to advance her son's military and political ambitions.

Then Churchill had some luck. His eponymous book on the recent campaign, *The Malakand Field Force,* had just appeared and attracted the favourable attention of no less a person than Lord Salisbury, a former friend of Lord Randolph and currently the Prime Minister. Lord Salisbury invited Churchill to a meeting which concluded with the Prime Minister's congratulations on the book and the request that if Churchill ever needed a personal favour the Prime Minister would be happy, indeed anxious, to help.

The English saying, 'It is not what you know, but whom you know' has rarely been more in evidence than in the Churchills' string-pulling in the spring of 1899. Everyone who was anyone had been approached, either by Lady Jennie or Winston, including the Commander-in-Chief, Lord Wolseley, the Adjutant-General of the Army, Sir Evelyn Wood, and the British Regent in Egypt, Lord Cromer. At first none of this proved helpful; the decision on who went up the Nile to Khartoum was Kitchener's, and he was not about to give in to pressure on behalf of young Churchill. The harder Churchill pushed, the more adamant was Kitchener's refusal.

However, the Prime Minister's personal intervention was another matter. Churchill asked that if the Prime Minister would kindly intervene and ask Kitchener to reconsider as the 21st Lancers, a cavalry regiment then in Egypt, had indicated that they could offer Churchill employment. The telegram was duly despatched, a carefully phrased missive, stating that while the Prime Minister would not dream of interfering with the Sirdar's prerogative over appointments if, in this particular situation the General could see his way clear...? The Prime Minister would, it was implied, find himself greatly obliged to General Kitchener and bear his name in mind...

To everyone's surprise, Churchill's chagrin, and Kitchener's credit, this intervention with its strong hint of future benefits did no good at all. Kitchener replied that his ranks were full and his appointments made – he had no need for the services of Mr Churchill. Impasse.

However, in giving such an abrupt reply to the Prime Minister's request, Kitchener went too far. His response had suddenly reminded the War Office that the British Army supplied a large part of the Nile force. Kitchener was, at this time, merely Sirdar of the Egyptian Army and it was none of his business who the War Office sent out to serve in British units. To demonstrate that the War Office alone would decide who officered its regiments in the field, Churchill's application was approved – but on certain terms.

These terms were laid out in Churchill's orders:

> 'You have been attached as a supernumerary lieutenant to the 21st Lancers for the Soudan campaign. You are to report at once to the Abassiyia Barracks, Cairo, to the Regimental Headquarters. It is understood that you will proceed at your own expense and in the event that you are killed or wounded in the impending operations, or for any other reason, no charge of any kind will fall on British Army funds.'

Churchill was not deterred by the blunt tone of this letter. His going to the Sudan that was the main thing, both as a cavalry officer and war correspondent. Clutching his letter he went to see his friend Oliver Borthwick, whose father owned the *Morning Post*, and came away with the commission to write a series of reports on the campaign at the rate of £15 ($60) per column. This was a very useful sum at the time and three times the rate Churchill had been paid for his Malakand despatches. That night he caught the boat train to France and six days later he was in Cairo.

This opportunity had come about through the death of a young cornet in the 21st Lancers, one of the British units deployed for Kitchener's expedition. His unfortunate demise provided everyone with an honourable way out of the impasse; the 21st Lancers had a vacancy – Lt Churchill of the 4th Hussars was on hand to fill it.

Within hours of reporting to the Colonel of the 21st Lancers in Cairo Churchill was embarked with the regiment on a Nile steamer. This went butting upstream towards Aswan and through the Nile cataracts to the Atbara, where Churchill finally caught up with the Army. It was August 15, 1898, just ten days before Kitchener began the final advance towards Khartoum.

By 1898 the Mahdi was long dead. *The Expected One* had expired in 1895, shortly after the death of Gordon and been replaced as leader of the Dervishes by the Kalifa Abdullah, a stern and equally charismatic leader who had summoned the entire Dervish host to resist this infidel invasion of the Sudan. This force had resisted the British advance with considerable courage but military equipment had improved remarkably in the last decade. The Dervish hordes, on foot or horseback, were really a medieval host, mostly armed with swords and spears and muskets and in no state to offer a great deal of resistance to Kitchener's force with its magazine rifles, machine-guns, field guns and Nile gunboats, all backed by a railway to ensure supply. A medieval army – some of the Kalifa's emirs wore chain mail dating from the Crusades – was about to collide with late 19th century technology and the result could not be long in doubt.

Kitchener's Army contained a large number of officers who would make their names – or meet their fate – in the Great War. Others present included Ian Hamilton, the commander at Gallipoli, Henry Rawlinson, later to command the Fourth Army during the Battle of the Somme and Lt David Beatty RN, who was to command the Cruiser

Squadron at the battle of Jutland in 1916. All these were added to Churchill's growing list of useful contacts and personal friends.

The 21st Lancers crossed the Nile on 16 August, made a nine-day march along the river to the Shabluka Cataract. This gave Churchill time to get to know his Troop and the Regiment, neither of which had made a favourable first impression. '*The 21st Lancers is not a good business*', he wrote to his mother, '*and on the whole I would prefer to be attached to the Egyptian cavalry staff.*'

Such an appointment to the Staff would have brought Churchill directly under Kitchener's command – and rather more to the point, under the Sirdar's eye, which Churchill was most anxious to avoid. Churchill was better off with the 21st Lancers and his opinion of them changed as time passed and he came to recognise their good qualities; by the time the Army reached Omdurman, Churchill was quite happy where he was.

Apart from the occasional glimpse of a Dervish horseman this advance from the Atbara was uncontested. Supported by gunboats towing the supply barges, the Army marched south and by 27 August were ready for the final march to Khartoum and Omdurman, just across the river, and the final encounter with the Dervish Army. The final advance from Shabluka began on 28 August, in full order of battle and in short stages of eight or ten miles a day until the enemy were first encountered in force on 1 September, 1898.

Churchill was riding with the forward cavalry screen when a subaltern came galloping back with the expected news, '*Enemy in Sight.*' Churchill rode forward and studied the ground to his front through field glasses but could see no sign of any enemy, except a long brown smear in the distance that might be a clump of thorn bushes. Then the Regimental Sergeant Major of the 21st Lancers came cantering back from the outpost line and told Churchill that this was indeed the enemy army – and '*quite a good Army*' at that.

Churchill was then summoned by the Commanding Officer and given a difficult, and very awkward assignment; he was to ride to the Sirdar and tell him that the enemy were in sight and coming on fast.

Since Churchill had been careful to keep out of Kitchener's way in the last week, this was a most unwelcome task but off he went, found Kitchener riding alone a few lengths in front of his Staff, and delivered the message.

'You say the Dervish Army is advancing' said Kitchener. ' How long have I got?'

' You have got at least an hour, sir', said Churchill, 'probably an hour and a half, even if they come on at the present rate.'

Kitchener digested this information and Churchill was dismissed without further comment; the Sirdar had more on his mind that morning than the fate of one cavalry lieutenant.

In fact the battle did not take place that day. The infantry came forward, brigade after brigade of British, Egyptian and Sudanese soldiers wheeling into line, scraping trenches with their bayonets or cutting down the thorn scrub to form *zaribas*, thick thorn fences which would repel the Dervish charge as much as their bayonets and massed rifle fire could. The Dervishes were famous and much respected in the British Army for twice during the Gordon Relief Expedition, at Tamai and Abu Klea, they had performed the feat of breaking the British square, an exploit that had defeated the armies of Napoleon. That, however, was before the advent of machine guns and magazine rifles, in the days of the single-shot Martini-Henry. Now that the British had the five-shot Lee-Metford rifle, those wild 'Fuzzy-Wuzzies' Kipling wrote about would not be allowed to charge home this time.

The day was already far advanced, however, and although the Dervish Army closed up and greeted the silent British formations with war cries and a great *feu de joie* of musketry, they then turned away. There was light skirmishing for the rest of the day but no onset; the armies settled down for the night, a few miles apart, lit fires and cooked an evening meal; the battle they had come here to fight would take place tomorrow.

Churchill enjoyed a better meal than most that night for as he was strolling along the banks of the Nile he was hailed from one of the Nile gunboats by Lt David Beauty who treated him to a chilled bottle of champagne. According to Churchill memoirs there was a general air of lighthearted anticipation in the British camp. As usual, no one expected to be killed; death was something that happened to the other fellow.

Certainly a few score of people might be killed or wounded but the mass slaughter, the almost-certainty of death or wounds that most of those officers and many of the men present on the banks of the Nile that night would experience within the next few years was so remote as to be unthinkable; the battle of Omdurman was the last big battle in a way of warfare that was rapidly going out of date. There were 60,000 armed Dervishes within three miles of the Anglo-Egyptian *zeriba*, odds in excess of three to one, but the Dervish Army would not have been out of place in the Middle Ages; in the face of modern weapons their destruction was certain if they pressed home their attack.

The camp was astir long before dawn and the 21st Lancers had saddled up and moved out to scout the enemy lines as dawn started to lighten the sky to the east. Churchill was put in charge of a scouting force of seven troopers and rode forward towards the ridge that concealed the presence and actions of the Dervish Army. It grew lighter as they rode and when they topped the ridge, moving cautiously anticipating an attack, visibility had risen to around 200 yards and was steadily increasing to a quarter of a mile, then half a mile and then to the horizon. Sitting his horse on the Jebel Surgham ridge, Churchill could see no sign of the Dervish host.

And then, as the sun lifted over the land, there they were. A vast dark mass lay on the brown face of the desert, a moving stain, glinting with steel and gay with flags, growing lighter and more colourful as the sun rose, a vast array, four or five miles wide and a mile deep, gradually separating into their regiments and battalions, each under the command of an emir. This army was coming on like a wave and Churchill, awed, stayed to watch it until the leading ranks were just a few hundred yards away and rifle and musket bullets were starting to spatter on the nearby rocks. It was time to pull back, but then a courier arrived with orders from the Sirdar: *'Remain as long as possible and report how the masses are moving.'*

Churchill and his patrol stayed out for another half hour, watching the Dervishes come up the slope of the Jebel Surgham and into sight of the main army which was now deployed behind its zeriba in a horseshoe formation on the bank of the Nile. Behind the lines of waiting watchful riflemen stood the guns; behind the guns, the gunboats all waiting for the order to open fire.

Churchill never forgot the sight of the Dervish Army; it was, he wrote later, like something out of the Bayeux Tapestry, a scene the Crusaders must have seen, a spectacle that would never be seen again. Then the batteries and gunboats began their cannonade and down went the Dervishes by the score and hundred under this hail of steel and high explosive – and still they came on, cheering, waving swords and spears, topped by a mass of colourful banners, and replying to this barrage with a storm of musketry which did little damage to the troops in the *zeriba* but wreathed their advancing ranks in thick white clouds of gunpowder smoke.

Nor was this all; Dervish cavalry was now active on the flanks and looked likely to encircle the watching picquets and cavalry scouts, so another messenger reached Churchill's position, telling him that the infantry were about to open fire and to pull back at once before they did so. Spurs were applied and the picquet was just back inside the zeriba when the British infantry began firing volleys into the Dervish ranks and the great slaughter of the day began. The Dervish Army mustered more than three times the force Kitchener commanded but this was not a battle between numbers; this was a battle between a medieval army and a modern force, between weapons of the Middle Ages – sword and spear – and late 19th century technology. In such a battle the odds lay with the modernists and the issue was not long in doubt.

The Kalifa's force came on and was blown away by artillery, machine gun fire and the rolling volleys of the British and Egyptian infantry; Dervish casualties exceed 12,000 – British losses, killed and wounded, barely reached 200.

The battle did not end without one historic, even traditional event, one harking back to former days of the *arme blanche* cavalry, a charge against a superior force by the 21st Lancers. The 21st Lancers may have entered this battle feeling they had something to prove; the latest and last cavalry regiment to enter the ranks of the British Army, they had never seen action and other regiments were prone to whisper that the motto of the 21st Lancers was '*Thou shalt not kill.*' The 21st Lancers were rather weary of this joke and when the chance came for close action, they were quick to take it.

During the main engagement in front of the *zariba*, the Lancers had been held on the left flank, guarding the approach from Omdurman. When the first Dervish attack had been beaten back the Lancers were ordered to move out and advance towards the city, discovering what forces stood between Kitchener's army and the city and brushing them out of the way if need be. The regiment swung into a column of troops and advanced over the top of the Jebel Surgham, from where they could see the walls and towers of Omdurman, six miles away across the flood plain. Churchill was commanding the last but one troop in the column as they came down the slope of the ridge and trotted towards Omdurman.

Churchill records that everyone in the regiment knew there must be a charge, that charging the enemy was what cavalry were for and the only reason they had come all this way – some 1500 miles from Cairo. The only question was whom they should charge. There were Dervishes, alone or in small groups, all over the plain, but nothing worthy of a charge until a larger body of enemy was noted some 300 yards away on their right flank.

There seemed to be around 150 Dervishes taking cover in a low depression or *nullah*, and they were clearly armed with rifles and muskets for bullets and musket balls began to spatter about the Lancer column – a few horses fell, a saddle or two was emptied – this enemy had to be avoided or engaged. The sensible approach to such harassing fire was either to gallop out of range and move on, or gallop away to a flank, dismount, and bring the Dervishes under carbine fire. Neither course appealed to the officers and men of the 21st Lancers.

The Colonel spoke briefly to the trumpeter at his side, the trumpet sounded '*Right Wheel into Line;*' within seconds all 16 Troops had wheeled round to face the Dervishes, set spurs and broken into a gallop. *'The 21ˢᵗ Lancers'* wrote Churchill *'were committed to their first charge in war.'*

The 21ˢᵗ Lancers was not a large force; when they opened this charge the regiment mustered just 310 officers and men, the men carrying lances, the officers drawn sabres. Churchill had previously reached the conclusion – probably after that skirmish in the Malakand – that if the fighting ever got to close quarters, it was better to be armed with a pistol than a sword and before coming out to Egypt had purchased the latest model of Mauser automatic. The problem now, as the regiment thundered down on the enemy, was to sheath his sabre and draw and cock the pistol. It is to the credit of Churchill's horsemanship that he managed to do both before the regiment, now in full career, reached the edge of the *nullah* and made a sudden and shocking discovery.

The hundred or so riflemen and musketeers they had seen already were only a portion of the enemy force; the nullah was now revealed as a steep-sided, shallow, river bed – like a sunken road, four or five feet deep, says Churchill – crammed with more than two thousand Dervishes, their packed ranks glittering with swords and spears as they rose to meet the British charge.

There was no time for hesitation. The Lancers galloped full tilt into the enemy, some jumping their horses from the edge of the nullah into the enemy ranks, others plunging down the slope, driving their lances into the first of the enemy and then drawing their sabres to cut their way through to the elusive safety of the open desert. Others were not so fortunate; they were brought to a halt by the sheer numbers of the enemy, dragged from their saddles and hacked to pieces.

When they thundered up to the *nullah*, Churchill's Troop was at the right of the line. They looked likely to overlap the enemy so they increased their speed and curved in to strike the enemy flank – at which point Churchill's account of the charge becomes understandably confused.

He recalls two 'blue men' immediately to his front and spurred his horse at the interval between them; they fire and kill the trooper riding at Churchill's side. Churchill's horse drops to the floor of the nullah and he finds himself surrounded by the enemy, dozens of them but not thickly packed together, though the troop on his left, commanded by Lt Julian Grenfell, is brought to a halt and suffers losses. Churchill's men are more fortunate; they spear or sabre their way through, their horses scrambling up the far side of the ditch onto the open desert.

All is not over for there are more Dervishes here and this is their kind of battle, not with and against technology but sword to sabre and spear to lance. One of these men flings himself on the ground before Churchill's cantering horse and prepares to hamstring it with a sword cut but Churchill swings away and leaning from the saddle fires two shots into him at a distance of a few yards. Then another swordsman appears, rushing in with uplifted sword and is shot down so close that he disappears under Churchill's horse. Then a Dervish emir gallops past, in chain mail and a brightly coloured tunic; Churchill fires at him and he turns aside. Churchill pulls his horse to a walk, and looks around.

Away to his left, forty or fifty yards distant, a mass of Dervishes is still engaged with the Lancers, probably with the survivors of Grenfell's troop. Behind him, on the near side of the nullah, some riflemen are aiming their rifles at him but the scattered Dervishes close by make no attempt to attack. Churchill stops his horse and discovers that he is completely alone; this will not do so he puts spurs to his horse yet again and gallops away for another two or three hundred yards – and finds his Troop, sitting on panting horses, drawn up in line and waiting for him. Other men arrive and within a few minutes the regiment is starting to reform.

Churchill and the Troop Serjeant Major conduct a quick roll call; the Troop appear to have lost three or four men and another half dozen men and a dozen horses are wounded, bleeding from spear thrusts or sword slashes. This is not too bad and the men grasp their weapons, ready and waiting to charge back again, asking permission to throw away their lances and use their swords. One sergeant, asked by Churchill if he has enjoyed his first charge replies: *'Well, I can't exactly say I enjoyed it, Sir, but I think I'll get more used to it next time.'*

This comment produced a laugh but the men's good humour did not last long; trailing across the desert from the *nullah* came a ghastly procession; wounded horses, some missing a hoof, men cut and slashed, some with Dervish weapons still embedded in their bodies, arms hacked, intestines protruding, voices moaning and screaming. The men had to be taken care of, the wounded horses despatched, any enemy resistance repulsed.

Reason also prevailed; the Colonel of the 21st Lancers suddenly recalled that his regiment had carbines, the trumpet sounded and taking the wounded along the regiment moved off at a smart clip and took up a position from which they could rake the nullah with fire; after a few minutes of this the Dervishes withdrew and within twenty minutes of hearing the *'Wheel into Line'* the 21st Lancers were breakfasting in the nullah among the bodies of the Dervish and Lancer dead.

Churchill was lucky to survive this charge. The 21st Lancers lost five officers and 66 men killed or wounded – a casualty rate in excess of 20 percent in an action that lasted less than five minutes; 119 horses were also lost. The bodies of the dead Lancers were so hacked about and mutilated as to be mostly unrecognisable – the cost of this somewhat pointless charge had been considerable.

Churchill's accounts of the Omdurman campaign were duly published in the *Morning Post* and well received in the UK. The Omdurman campaign also provided the basis for Churchill's next book, *The River War* which also went down well with the public but was much less appreciated in the Army. Churchill had been with the Expedition for less than a month and the charge of the 21st Lancers, while dramatic and dangerous, had lasted less than half an hour; the two together hardly provided enough material to support a book, so Churchill elected to expand the coverage, including a complete account of the British involvement in the Sudan leading up to the battle at Omdurman.

That event then led to Churchill making some outspoken criticisms of Kitchener, not least the latter's neglect of the Dervish wounded after the battle but also over certain other actions, including the destruction of the Mahdi's tomb in Khartoum and the Sirdar's attempt to turn the Mahdi's skull into an inkwell, an action widely regarded as both barbaric and quite unsuitable behaviour in a British general officer. Naturally enough, this criticism of a senior and victorious general by a young cavalry officer was not received well among the higher ranks of the Army. Even so, *The River War* was completed by July 1899 and published to considerable public acclaim in the following November.

By that time Churchill, now aged 24, had come to two decisions. The first was to leave the Army and seek a career in politics. The second, following the critical and financial success of his first two histories, was to support himself, in and out of Parliament, by authorship and journalism. He decided to sail to South Africa where yet another war – a much more serious and dangerous war than anything offered by the Nile campaign – had recently broken out between the British and the Boers.

4. Fame

1899

*'Throughout the vast sub-continent, every man's hand
was against his brother and the British Government
could, for the moment, be sure of nothing
beyond the gunshot of the Navy.'*

Winston S. Churchill

Churchill's motivation for leaving the Army seems to have been
inspired by two basic causes: ambition and money. His brief military
career, while varied and active, had not actually involved this young
officer spending much time on regimental duties. Indulgent colonels,
social connections, the actions of his mother and relentless pursuit of
self-interested military adventures had frequently taken Churchill
away from his regiment and enabled him to participate in some
dangerous campaigns. This was highly commendable in a young
cavalry officer but, clearly, the humdrum routine of life as a regimental
officer in barracks was not to Churchill's taste at all.

Although Churchill kept up a lifelong connection with the 4th Hussars and visited it in camp and field whenever the opportunity allowed even as Prime Minister, all the evidence suggests that, in the end, the connection was more highly regarded by the regiment than by its most famous member. When the time came for Churchill to consider his future, regimental ties were quickly broken.

The second chronic problem was money. The Churchills, in spite of their aristocratic connections, were not at all rich. Churchill had to live on his pay as a regimental officer around 14 shillings (70p), say $3, a day, plus an allowance of £500 ($2,000) a year from his mother, paid quarterly. This was not nearly enough to cover his costs in Mess or provide for such necessary extras as polo ponies, leave to the UK, gambling and champagne, all of which were part of the life of any cavalry officer in the glory days of Empire.

On the other hand, his journalism had proved highly lucrative and the books, while equally useful in floating his bank account off the financial rocks, had also brought him a gratifying amount of public attention and honed his already sound writing skills. Churchill thoroughly enjoyed his growing reputation as a writer and adventurer, a fame that grew after the Nile campaign when he found everyone, especially young society ladies, anxious to hear about the battle and especially about the charge.

On his way back to Britain from Cairo Churchill considered his future. His writings had in three years brought him in five times as much money as he had been paid by the Army for a great deal of sometimes dangerous work. When he considered all his options the choice was clear and stark; he could stay in the Army and find what action he could while veering wildly between affluence and debt, or leave and take his chance as a writer and politician.

This latter aim, of following in his father's footsteps, had never been too far from his thoughts. He had kept in contact with his father's many friends and former colleagues, and felt sure that his growing reputation would gain him a Parliamentary seat in a Tory constituency whenever he asked for it.

That settled, Churchill decided on his immediate course of action. He would return to India and devote his energies to helping the regimental team with the Polo Tournament in February 1899. He would 'send in his papers' – the current term for resigning his commission. He would tell his mother that her allowance might end – thus ensuring her support for his intention of leaving the Army. He would finish his book on the recent campaign and expand his journalistic contacts. Finally, he would explore the possibilities of finding a Parliamentary seat. By December 1898, Churchill was due to return to India; before leaving he started putting these ideas in train.

Finding a Parliamentary seat appeared all too easy. In November 1898, soon after his return from Egypt, Churchill visited the Central Office of the Conservative Party and enquired about the possibility of obtaining a seat. The Party Manager, a Mr Middleton, had known Lord Randolph and said that he foresaw no difficulties in finding his son and heir a suitable constituency. This was very gratifying, but then Mr Middleton moved on to the sordid subject – money.

At the turn of the 19th century, Members of Parliament were not paid, hence Churchill's need to balance politics with profitable journalism. However, it transpired that MPs were also expected to disburse funds in the form of contributions to local charities and good causes within their constituencies, contributions that in some cases reached £1,000 a year.

This news dismayed Churchill as much as the information that the would-be Member had no money dismayed Mr Middleton. However, further discussion revealed that there were exceptions to this rule; while safe seats were expensive, marginal constituencies were far less costly and Liberal strongholds positively cheap. Somewhere or other there would be a place for Winston Churchill.

This visit to the Central Office led to yet another expansion of Churchill's activities – public speaking. In an age before radio or TV there was a constant demand for speakers, willing to go about the country and encourage Party members, and Churchill was quickly signed up to deliver a speech to a Party gathering in Bristol. He was accompanied there by a political correspondent from the Morning Post, his speech of some 20 minutes duration, partly on the evils of socialism, was well received by the audience and hailed in the leader columns of the *Morning Post* as signalling the arrival of a new star in the political firmament. Well content with the progress of his plans, Churchill departed for India.

Churchill's last months in India were crowned with sporting success; the 4th Hussars won the Polo Cup. That done and Churchill's resignation accepted, he set out for home, his military career over – or so it seemed.

On the outward and homeward voyages, and in what time could be spared from polo in India, Churchill had been working away steadily at *The River War*. On his return to Britain, another activity intervened; it transpired that one of the Members for Oldham, a two-member constituency in Lancashire was ill and wanted to retire. The remaining Member, a Mr Ascroft, wanted a new running mate and invited Churchill to contest the seat. Oldham, a cotton town, was a winnable seat so Churchill was delighted to accept – and then came tragedy when Mr Ascroft died. This turned out to be advantageous for Churchill, who was promptly invited to take over the empty seat and contest it at the by-election.

During the campaign, Churchill made a costly tactical mistake. The Tory Government, then in office were urging a Bill – the Clerical Tithes Bill – designed to ease the poverty of the Anglican clergy. This Bill was opposed by the Non-Conformist congregations which were strong in the Lancashire cotton towns and Churchill was advised by his local advisers that he could only ensure his election if he promised to oppose the Bill if elected. Churchill had no personal opinions on the Clerical Tithes Bill; he had barely heard of it before rushing up to Oldham to start campaigning. He therefore agreed to his advisers' proposals and declared he would oppose the Bill.

This, said Churchill, was a frightful mistake. The Tory Government were taunted in Parliament with the fact that their new star was already in opposition to their policies and the Liberals in Oldham redoubled their efforts to gain the seat – and were successful. Both Tory candidates were defeated, and the blame for this disaster fell squarely on Winston Churchill. Mr Balfour, then the Leader of the House, remarked to his colleagues that, *'I thought he (Churchill) was a man of promise but now I see he is a man of promises.'*

Somewhat deflated by this crushing and unexpected reverse, Churchill returned to London and *The River War*, which had now expanded to two volumes. This book, his *magnum opus* so far, had reached the proof stage when war again intervened, this time in South Africa.

The origins of the South African or Boer War can be traced back to the arrival of the Europeans in Southern Africa in the late 17th century. The first to arrive were the Dutch, who soon left the coast to trek inland. They were followed by the British, who were principally motivated by the need to establish a port on the Cape route to India. However, as elsewhere, the need to ensure the security of the port led the British to incursions into the hinterland and eventual collision with the Dutch farmers who by then had colonised much of the Cape and Natal. The two people did not agree on many matters, most particularly on religion and the treatment of the native population whom the Dutch – the Boers – treated as slaves, warring on the interior tribes, stirring up wars with the Zulu and Matabele people. This conflict provided the Boers with land but inhibited the British attempts at peaceful settlement and trade.

There was also a political dimension. The Boers had little contact with the Government in Holland; they were a free people, living off the land, running their own affairs, beholden to no man. The British, on the other hand, were controlled by the Government in Britain, which sent out civil servants, administrators and military garrisons, all of which interfered with the habits and practises of the local people. Eventually, unable to endure this constant interference from the *roineks* – the rednecks or British settlers – the Boers inspanned their oxen and began a Great Trek away from the British, heading north across the Vaal river, away from the British in the Cape Colony and Natal, and established two Boer Republics, in the Transvaal and the Orange Free State.

However, conflict continued, largely over the issue of the native tribes. In 1877, claiming there was anarchy in the Transvaal, Britain annexed the Boer Republic, declaring it a colony in 1879. In that year there was further trouble, this time in Zululand. This last action was a step too far. In 1880 the Boers rebelled, declared the Transvaal a republic and thrashed the British Army at a series of battles during what came to be called the First Boer War, culminating in the major defeat at Majuba Hill in February 1881.

This defeat brought about the end of the war but not the end of the dispute. The issue of sovereignty was still unresolved but essentially, the Transvaal remained a colony but one which the Boers ran more or less as they pleased – peace was maintained but remained fragile. The issue was compounded in the 1880s by the discovery of gold around Johannesburg in the Transvaal. This brought an influx of mostly British foreigners – *uitlanders* or outlanders – who were denied any form of political say by the Boers, but soon showed themselves adept at making money and dominating affairs in Johannesburg. Then came the painful incident of the Jameson Raid, an attempted coup sponsored by Cecil Rhodes, and tensions mounted,

Finally, in 1899, the Boer leader, Paul Kruger, issued an ultimatum to the British Government; Britain was to abandon any claim to sovereignty over the Transvaal and remove her garrisons. This ultimatum was to expire on 11 October, 1899, and when it expired without the desired response the Boers at once attacked their British neighbours in Natal and the Cape Colony.

Inevitably, the British were not ready. The scattered garrisons dotted about South Africa could muster less than 15,000 men, most of them infantry, without much in the way of artillery and lacking cavalry. The Boers could muster two or three times that force, and although irregular, the Boers had always been organised for war, mustering their menfolk in locally-raised bodies of well-mounted, well-armed horse known as 'commandos.' These commandos could move fast and hit hard and when they met the British in battle proved themselves both hardy soldiers and excellent shots. The British therefore began this South African War in a traditional fashion, with a series of disasters.

Churchill sailed for South Africa on 11 October, 1899, embarking on the SS *Dunotter Castle* immediately after receiving his appointment as war correspondent from the *Morning Post*. This appointment was a considerable advance on his previous efforts; he was now on the newspaper staff, not merely a freelance, paid by the space he filled. He was retained on a minimum four months' contract at the rate of £250 ($1,000) a month, plus all expenses and complete freedom to go where he wanted and write what he pleased.

On the ship taking him to the Cape was the designated commander of the British forces in South Africa, the hero of the Zulu War of 1879, General Sir Redvers Buller VC and his Staff, and during the two week voyage Churchill made many useful contacts and forged some useful friendships.

There was nothing else to do in the days before wireless communication. Those on board were completely cut off from events in South Africa and gradually convinced themselves that the war would probably be over by the time they docked in Table Bay. This disappointing if comforting illusion was shattered after about a week when a ship was seen on the horizon, heading north, probably from South Africa. Course was altered, flags hoisted and as the ships passed each other the tramp steamer hung a blackboard over the rail, informing the soldiery that there had been a number of battles in South Africa and the general commanding the British forces there, Major General Penn Symons, had been killed.

This was grave news. Generals are not supposed to get killed and if one had indeed lost his life so quickly, perhaps the Boers would not be easily defeated after all. The ship docked in Capetown after dark some days later and the staff and troops swarmed anxiously ashore, accompanied by Churchill, who was equally anxious to find the war and file his first report.

The news was bad. The Boers had invaded Natal and driven the British back from the town of Dundee. Although the Boers had then been defeated at the battle of Talana Hill, they had managed to kill Penn-Symons and drive most of his army into the town of Ladysmith where they had joined the next commander, General Sir George White, who had plenty of men – around 12,000 when the remains of Penn Symons' force were included, plus a brigade of cavalry and around 50 guns.

The war had also slowed; the British were anxious to defend certain towns, Ladysmith, Kimberley and Mafeking, and the Boers equally anxious to take them. While the British stayed in these towns the Boers were checked; when the British moved out to drive them away, the results were disastrous. At Belmont, Graspan and the Modder river, the Boers shot down a great number of British soldiers and then rode away, unscathed, to fight another day. Some fresh thinking was required and Buller was the man chosen to provide it.

This war was over 1,000 miles away to the north of Capetown, on the boarders of Natal and the Transvaal. To get to it, Churchill had first to take the train to East London on the east coast of Africa, and travel from there by ship and in a heavy gale to reach the city of Durban, the main base for operations in Natal. Churchill arrived there several days before the Commanding General and his Staff.

Durban was calm but here, closer to the war, it was very clear that all was not going well. The Boer *commandos* were a fully mounted force and used this mobility – and their skill with weapons – to either harass scattered British outposts and columns or combine rapidly to defeat any larger force sent against them. They had already succeeded in cutting off several towns and winning that series of small battles and were to inflict even more severe losses on the ponderous British forces in the weeks ahead. In one week alone – later known as Black Week – between 10-17 December, the Boers defeated the British at Magersfontein, the Modder River, and Colenso.

Churchill quickly absorbed all this and sent several despatches to his paper before setting out again, this time for Pietermaritzburg, where Churchill found the hospitals full of wounded and then to the furthest British outpost, the railway junction at Estcourt, where he encountered an old acquaintance from the Malakand expedition, Captain Alymer Haldane.

Churchill had been hoping to get into the besieged town of Ladysmith but this was not completely cut off so he decided to take a trip up the railway line, in the company of Captain Haldane who was commanding a recently constructed armoured train with which he proposed making an armed reconnaissance to the north.

Churchill's position – was he soldier or civilian? – seems to have been a little confused at this time. He had resigned his commission in the 4th Hussars but he remained on the list of retired officers. In spite of his civilian status and journalistic credentials Churchill was, as always, willing and eager to take charge of events – and he was armed with that Mauser pistol he had carried at Omdurman. Thus equipped, he joined the train and on 15 November they set out for the North.

The railway line north of Estcourt did not run very far, only about 14 miles and most of this was in Boer territory. The countryside appeared deserted, at least for a while, but presently groups of horsemen appeared on the nearby hills and a spattering of bullets rattled off the armour plate of the engine and carriages. Should the Boers close on the track and lift a few rails the train could be cut off, so the order was given to withdraw to Estcourt. The train headed back at a smart clip and was doing some 40 miles an hour when it came to a bend and some of the leading carriages ran off the track.

The impact was considerable. Several soldiers were injured in the crash and the Boers quickly closed in and brought the remainder under heavy and accurate fire. Haldane and Churchill conferred and it was decided that Haldane should organise the defence while Churchill examined the damage to the train and track and decided what to do next.

It soon appeared that the track was intact and the derailment had been caused by excessive speed rather than enemy action. The engine, which was in the middle of the train, was still on the rails and only two overturned carriages were blocking the way out. If these could be moved, a withdrawal was possible. A party of troops was mustered and working in the open under rifle fire, Churchill succeeded in getting one carriage dragged clear and the engine steamed up to butt another one aside. This was done but unfortunately the carriages still on the rails could not be dragged past and had to be uncoupled. Even so, with the wounded carried on the engine and coal tender and the rest of the party moving on foot, sheltering behind the engine and keeping up a steady fire, the withdrawal to Estcourt began with Churchill in the engine compartment, controlling the driver and keeping the engine at walking pace.

Even this proved too fast. Before long the engine was around 300 yards ahead of the soldiers and pulling steadily away. Churchill therefore ordered the driver to stop the engine and, getting out, went back on foot to urge the soldiers forward. This again brought him under direct fire and he took shelter by crossing the embankment and was heading for the cover of a small hut when he was overtaken by a Boer horseman, who covered him with a rifle and ordered him to stop.

Churchill reached for his pistol, determined to kill this man and continue the escape, only to find that in the scramble to right the carriages and organise the escape, the pistol had vanished. The Boer was meanwhile looking at him over rifle sights from forty yards away – there was nothing to do but put up his hands and surrender. Three years later Churchill was to learn that his captor, the rifleman on the horse, was General Louis Botha, one of the senior Boer commanders, a man who later became one of Churchill's closest friends.

Standing helpless on the *veldt* Churchill was joined before long by the remainder of the foot party. He was also in a certain amount of jeopardy; Churchill was a civilian but he was wearing parts of his old Army uniform and had been observed by his captors taking part in the defence of the train. Civilians who take part in military engagements can be regarded as *franc-tireurs* – irregulars - and shot out of hand. Churchill feared this might indeed be his fate when he was ordered away from the rest of the prisoners and his fate debated by the Boers.

Fortunately, the Boer War was not conducted on strict military lines; Churchill's status as a war correspondent was accepted and he rejoined the other prisoners. *'The Boers,'* he wrote later, ' *were the most good hearted enemy I have ever fought against, in the four continents in which it has been my fortune to see active service.'*

While the rest of the armoured train steamed back to Estcourt, Churchill, Haldane and the surviving soldiers were taken, by train or on foot, on a three day journey back to a prison camp in the Transvaal capital, Pretoria. It seemed that this latest venture was going to end badly for Churchill; his journalistic career would not flourish if he spent the rest of this war in a Boer prison camp.

The officer prisoners were housed in the State Model Schools in Pretoria, in adequate comfort but closely guarded. This confinement did not suit the prisoners who were planning to escape as soon as they reached Pretoria. This would not be easy, for Pretoria was a Boer town and the nearest safety was 250 miles away to the west in the Portuguese colony of Mozambique.

There were about 60 officers in this prison and various escape plans were put together and rejected. Even at night the camp was well lit and surrounded by guards but after a few days in was noted that there was one spot on the surrounding wall where a patch of deep shadow could be exploited if the guards patrolling on the far side should happen to look the other way. Churchill was also complaining loudly to his captors that, as a civilian, he should not be confined at all. At first the Boers, knowing he had taken part in the fight around the train, fully intended to keep him in captivity but eventually appeared willing to release him; whether they would have done so remains unknown as before any final decision was reached, Churchill escaped.

Churchill had intended to go over the wall accompanied by Lts Haldane and Brockie, the latter a South African who spoke Afrikaans and several native languages fluently. On 11 December, the three concealed themselves in a latrine close to the wall, observing the sentries and awaiting their moment. When it came, the two sentries stopping for a chat, Churchill was the first over the wall and taking shelter in the undergrowth of the garden beyond. Then the sentries resumed their patrol and his colleagues could not join him.

Nor could Churchill scramble back; his choice was either to walk around to the main gate and give himself up or make the escape bid on his own, without a map or any knowledge of the local area or languages. Given Churchill's temperament this decision did not take long. He strolled out of the garden, passed within a few feet of the sentries on the main gate and made his way into Pretoria.

Churchill was without map or compass, but he knew that the Delgoa Bay Railway ran due east from Pretoria to the Mozambique port of Lorenco Marques. That was 300 miles away, too far to walk, too much ground to cover without hope of detection. Churchill therefore resolved to find the railway line and somehow board a train. He eventually found the railway line and walked along it, discovering that every bridge was guarded. He had been walking for about two hours, diverting off the track at every bridge and wayside halt, when he heard a train coming up behind him and managed to scramble on board. Once on board he concealed himself deep among a consignment of empty coal sacks and went to sleep as the train rattled slowly to the east.

Churchill decided to leave the train before daylight; the hunt for the escaped prisoner would now be underway and he needed to hide and find some water before moving on, nor was he entirely sure that he was in fact on an east-bound train; there was another line to Pietermaritzburg and he might have inadvertently got on that. He therefore flung himself off the train and took shelter in a wood, very relieved when the sun rose in the east, high above the track.

Churchill's intention was to make the rest of his escape in the same fashion. He would travel by train at night, getting off in daylight to shelter and find water; apart from a bar of chocolate he had no food. In this way he hoped to cover sixty or seventy miles every night; should the trains be searched this would either be in daylight when he was not aboard or at some station at night when he stood a fair chance of slipping away in the darkness. That decided, he spent that day close to the track and at dusk he went onto the railway line and waited for a train.

Hours past and no trains came by. Eventually he decided to walk east and gain what distance he could but this soon proved difficult. Every bridge and crossing was guarded and he was forced to wade rivers and make wide diversions; very little ground was covered to the east. Sometime after midnight Churchill decided to head for some fires he could see far away from the track; these he took to be the fires of native *kraals* where he might hope to find assistance.

It took some hours to reach these fires which turned out to be the furnace fires of a coal mine but by that time Churchill was too tired and hungry to care. He went up to the front door of a house and demanded admittance, declaring to the occupant that he was a burgher who had fallen from a train while en route to join his unit. He was admitted …and he was lucky.

The occupant of the house was the mine manager, Mr John Howard, an Englishman but a Transvaal citizen. Had Churchill knocked on any other house in the area he would have been recaptured at once but Howard agreed to help him, gave him a much-needed meal and sheltered him that night in the depths of the coal mine, which was well supplied with rats. In this Howard was aided by the mine engineer, Mr Dewsnap, who came from Oldham and told Churchill that '*They'll all vote for you next time.*'

Churchill was well aware that Howard and Dewsnap were taking a considerable risk in helping him. Howard, as a Trasvaaler, would certainly have been shot as a traitor had his part in Churchill's escape been discovered. Churchill urged them to find him a horse and a revolver and let him take his chances of an escape across country. His helpers, who now included two Scots miners, flatly refused. There was, it appeared, a great hue and cry in the surrounding area, with parties of Boers searching every barn and wood in the hope of finding the escaped Churchill – and the sum of £25 would be paid to anyone who brought him in – dead or alive.

Churchill stayed in the mine for several days; luckily he had no fear of rats and had candles and books so the time passed without undue discomfort: The mine was not in operation so no workers came down to disturb or find him, and on the third day Mr Howard informed him that a wool train was leaving for the frontier at Komati Poort and then on Lorenco Marques. They had arranged a space among the wool bales for Churchill; with any luck another day's travel would find him in safety.

So it turned out. Churchill was smuggled onto the train at 2:00am on 19 November; he had a revolver, two roast chickens, some slices of meat, a melon and three bottles of cold tea and a hiding place deep among the wool bales. The train pulled away at daylight and travelled east all that day, stopping for the night in a siding. There was no search and moving on again next day the train reached the border at Komati Poort that evening, waiting there for several tense hours before moving on again.

Tucked into his hiding place Churchill was still not entirely sure that he was in neutral territory, but the sight of Portuguese uniforms on wayside stations soon put his mind at rest, and as the train rumbled on towards Lorenco Marques he celebrated his escape by sitting on top of the truck, yelling with delight and firing his revolver into the air. That night he dined in the British Consulate in Lorenco Marques and two days later he arrived back in Durban aboard the steamship *Induna* – and found himself famous.

As the *Induna* sailed in, the ships already in harbour broke out flags and sounded their sirens. Bands played, crowds embarked in little boats came out to greet the *Induna*, demanding a sight of the returning hero. When he got ashore Churchill was hoisted on the shoulders of the mob and borne through the streets to the Town Hall where he was obliged to give a speech. The Port Admiral and the Garrison Commander arrived to shake his hand and sheaves of telegrams and cables flooded in from every part of the world, all full of gratifying praise.

It might all have gone to his head but Churchill was never over-impressed with acclaim. He enjoyed it but it did not turn him away from his previous path. He had come to South Africa to report on the War and this he proceeded to do. A day after arriving in Durban he was back with the Army.

5. The Young Politician

1900 – 1911

*'Youth seeks adventure; journalism requires advertisement.
Certainly I had found both; I became for the time quite famous.'*

Winston S. Churchill

One of the most curious aspects of Winston Churchill's early career is how short these various, dramatic episodes that marked his life actually were. The brief extent of his time with the Malakand Field Force and during the Omdurman campaign have already been noted and a similar short period embraces his time in South Africa. Churchill arrived in Capetown in November 1899, and was back in England, basking in public adulation, in July 1900, after an absence of just over eight months. This absence might have been even shorter had he elected to return to Britain on the high tide of fame that followed his escape from Pretoria and used that public attention to further his political ambition.

In the event, Churchill returned to his journalistic duties in the field and, as in the Sudan, enlivened his reports with some critical, perceptive and in certain military circles most unwelcome comments on the tactics, strategy and competence of the various British commanders. He noted, for example, that in the face of modern firepower, frontal assaults would always be repulsed – but also that the Boers' horse-borne mobility made attempts at outflanking their positions virtually impossible.

The only viable policy, Churchill declared, was to bring out a mass of troops and grind the Boer Republics down in a campaign of attrition. The fact that this policy was both correct and the one eventually adopted under Lord Roberts and Kitchener, after Redvers Buller had been removed from command, did not prevent Churchill coming under considerable criticism at the time. His military career had peaked at the rank of lieutenant, and criticism of commanding generals from a very junior officer – and one no longer in the Service – was not the best way for Churchill to make friends in high places. This thought, if it ever occurred to him, did not bother Churchill at all.

As well as representing the *Morning Post*, Churchill now applied for a commission in one of the irregular cavalry units rapidly springing up to counter the Boer Commandos and was restored to the Army as a lieutenant in the South African Light Horse. This was a well mounted and fast moving unit commanded by Colonel the Hon. Julian Byng, a well-regarded officer who was to command the Canadian Corps with some distinction in the First World War. Byng appointed Churchill Assistant-Adjutant of the Regiment and allowed him to go where he wanted when the unit was not actually on operations. Churchill took full advantage of this concession and saw more service at the front. During his time with the South African Horse Churchill took part in the relief of Ladysmith and was at both the battle at Spion Kop and the taking of Pretoria.

During some of these adventures he was joined, albiet briefly, by his brother Jack. On 12 February , during an action against the Boers at Hussar Hill, Jack was wounded by a bullet in the leg. Churchill was present and carried his brother off the battlefield. Jack then had to be evacuated under fire, first to a nearby casualty clearing station and then onto a hospital ship moored at Durban. This proved the occasion for a family reunion for Lady Jennie was on board this ship, running the wards as hospital matron, having persuaded an American millionaire to buy and equip the ship while she rounded up a staff of trained nurses and led them to South Africa. Her ship had just arrived in Durban and the first casualty to come on board was Lady Jennie's younger son. Winston soon arrived as well and the family stayed together for some weeks.

The fall of Pretoria on 5 June, 1900, led many people, Boers as well as British, to suppose that the South Africa War was over. In fact the Boer forces continued 'on commando' and kept up the struggle with another two years of irregular warfare. In June 1900 it seemed that peace, if not currently on offer, was at least just around the corner. This being so, Churchill returned to his long term strategy and, with an election looming, decided to return to the UK and restart his political career.

Churchill refers to this election as a 'Khaki Election.' The issue that provoked it was indeed the progress of the South African War and the desire of the Conservative Party to profit from this apparent victory at Pretoria while it was still fresh in the public mind. It was also considered necessary to get a new popular mandate before proceeding with the next step in South Africa, the annexation of the defeated Boer republics of the Transvaal and the Orange Free State. There was considerable public opposition to this measure and the best way to resolve it was by a fresh election.

Churchill was again the Tory candidate for Oldham. When he went up there to start his campaign, he was able to tell the full, thrilling story of his escape from Pretoria to an entranced electorate and give the names of his helpers in the coal mine – which was safely now in British hands. At one meeting, when he mentioned the local man, Mr Dewsnap, as one of his gallant helpers, the cry went up *'His wife's in the gallery'* and Churchill's fame and newfound popularity in the constituency led to the anticipation of certain victory and a solid majority. Mr Chamberlain, then party leader came up himself to campaign on Churchill's behalf and Winston was duly elected on the day – but by the slender margin of just 230 votes.

Churchill was just 26 years old when he became the MP for Oldham in 1900. He was to remain in Parliament for the next 50 years and serve in every office, his career peaking with his appointment of Prime Minister in the hard years between 1940-1945. Even so he rarely enjoyed the amount of adulation that followed his return from South Africa and his subsequent election at Oldham. A popular figure, he was sent about the country to speak for other candidates and as a result of his charisma quite a lot of local electoral victories followed in his wake. He was clearly seen as a great political asset and could expect early promotion to some junior ministerial rank when Parliament reassembled.

There remained the problem of money. MP's were not paid but neither were they unduly detained by their duties in the House; indeed, being a Member of Parliament was generally regarded as a part-time job for all those outside the Cabinet. It was generally thought, by the general public as well as by the Members, that regular experience of daily affairs outside politics enriched the House with a wealth of relevant, up-to-date knowledge of events in the world outside. In 1900 the notion of the 'professional politician' had not yet been thought of – and can still be seen as a very mixed blessing by the electorate

Churchill now had three sources of income – lecturing, authorship, and journalism – and he fully intended to devote at least as much time to these as to Parliamentary business. For the moment he was flush with funds; *The River War* had now been published and done very well, the sales greatly aided by his sudden burst of public acclaim. The publication of two books of correspondence on the South African War – *London to Ladysmith* and *Ian Hamilton's March* – plus his untouched salary as war correspondent for the *Morning Post* had increased his bank balance to more than £4,000 ($16,000) – considerable wealth in 1900 but a sum Churchill hoped to increase substantially in the immediate future by a string of speaking engagements in Britain and the US.

After the election, Parliament did not reassemble until 3 December, and then only for the election of a new Speaker and to hear the Queen's Speech – a speech which is actually written by the Prime Minister, outlining the Government's programme for the coming session. This was followed by a week of debate before the House broke up for the Christmas recess, a time which was largely devoted to the situation in South Africa. Churchill might have had something to say on this issue and been listened to with attention but he was not present. On 1 December he had sailed for the United States on a lecture tour.

This absence from Parliament so soon after his election may seem to indicate a cavalier, even disrespectful, attitude towards his constituents, his fellow Members, and the House itself but no one appears to have thought so at the time. In absenting himself from the House to fill a prior engagement, Churchill was merely acting in line with his current priorities. He had a Parliamentary seat – now he must find the means to support himself.

Fame is fleeting, not least in the days before radio and television, and Churchill was well advised to take full advantage of the publicity accruing from his exploits in South Africa before some fresh excitement drove him from public memory. Immediately after the election he had undertaken an extensive speaking tour around the United Kingdom and after three months his bank balance had been augmented by a further £3,782 (say $15,000), a substantial sum at the turn of the twentieth century – amounting to around $250,000 dollars in today's rate of exchange – and a good return for three months work at any time. The problem was that Churchill enjoyed high living; dinners, champagne, gambling, clothes and not least the requirements of his mother, sent the money out almost as fast as it came in.

Some of this money was now to be invested in a further round of speaking engagements in America, where British policy in South Africa was under attack. While Churchill had been listened to with respect in the UK and ended his speeches to generous applause, his US tour did not go so well. Churchill seems to have been surprised at the reception accorded to his views on the Empire and the South African War, though in places like Boston and Philadelphia where the Irish Americans had no love of any Englishman and strongly supported the Boers, hostility should have been expected. Nor did Churchill get on well with one of his hosts, Vice President Theodore Roosevelt – who became President shortly afterwards, following the assassination of President William McKinley.

The roots of Roosevelt's antagonism towards the young Churchill are obscure – perhaps it is no more than the fact that Roosevelt did not take to Churchill, though this is surprising since both men were adventurers and might be thought to have a lot in common – indeed, Roosevelt's daughter said later that the main reason for her father's animus was that the two men 'were so alike.' Whatever the reason, Roosevelt maintained his hostility to Churchill for decades and avoided his company whenever possible. Others were more accommodating, including famous people like the author Mark Twain, who presided at Churchill's opening address in New York City, and signed all thirty volumes of his collected works, on Tom Sawyer and Huckleberry Finn and his river boat life, for Churchill's benefit.

In spite of such a mixed reception the tour augmented Churchill's coffers by another substantial sum. In a rare burst of financial wisdom, on returning to the UK Churchill confided most of his recent earnings from lectures and journalism – which now amounted to around $750,000 in modern money, into the care of the financier Sir Ernest Cassel – and a close friend of his mother. This sum, and the dividends accruing from it should have provided Churchill with a more than adequate income but he continued to indulge his expensive tastes and this capital asset was gradually consumed.

For the moment though, his finances in good order and his strategy in place, he entered Parliament and began his new career. He made his maiden speech in the House of Commons on 18 February, 1901, just four days after taking his seat in spite of the convention that obliged new Members to wait a few months before expressing an opinion, and the advice of more experienced Members, that a first speech, which, by long tradition was listened to without interruption, should be on some uncontroversial issue.

Instead, Churchill spoke on the highly charged issue of the South African War, which had again flared up, arguing that some sensible accommodation with the Boer Republics, rather than their total suppression, was the best way to bring this tragic and unnecessary war to an end. This view met with general acclaim, especially from the Opposition benches.

While Churchill had been in North America, Queen Victoria had died and Edward VII now sat on the throne of his ancestors. The Edwardian Age, briefer and less glorious than the previous one, was to end in the disaster of the First World War and be dogged by a series of steps that led towards that fatal conflagration. In spite of his youth – at least in Parliamentary terms – Churchill was to play a full part in these proceedings and was an established member of the Government long before the Great War began.

Churchill's fairly rapid progress up the political ladder can be attributed at least partly to his father's posthumous reputation - which seems to have exceeded that which Lord Randolph enjoyed in his lifetime. That said, Churchill's oratory, if still in experimental form, was clearly impressive and attracted favourable notice in the House and in the Press – though here again many of these notices recall the manner and delivery of Churchill's father.

Apart from mere oratory, there were some burning issues. Churchill had learned from the original Oldham debacle that it was unwise to go against the policy of his Party, but he did not hesitate to disagree or speak out when he felt that Party policy needed attention or correction. Churchill soon found himself at odds with the majority of his Party over the conduct of the South African War; he admired the Boers and thought that they deserved to be treated with consideration and respect, though he also believed that they should first be defeated in the field.

Churchill was never the complete 'Party Man;' when it came to the point on some serious issue, some matter of principle, he went his own way, *coute que coute*. Indeed, his political career had hardly began when he began to drift away from the central tenets of Conservatism finding much to admire in the Liberal programme and cultivating a dislike of the rabid jingoism he detected in certain aspects of the Conservative programme, not least in the Party's attitude towards the Boers. Also, in spite of the early problem he had encountered during his first attempt at election, he failed to grasp the importance of Party loyalty: anyone can support their Party when it is clearly right – an elected MP is expected to support his Party when he believes it is wrong and argue the case internally.

At this time, Churchill's political attitudes were unformed and were not unlike those held in political circles before the 'Glorious Revolution' of 1688 and the subsequent establishment of parties under Walpole. Before that time, the terms 'Whig' and 'Tory' had simply indicated people who shared similar views on particular issues – there were no 'Parties' and no 'Party Line' as such. MP's therefore felt no inhibition towards being Tory on some issues and Whig (or Liberal) on others, choosing to take their own course on which issues they supported or opposed.

Those days of Parliamentary independence were long over by 1900, but signs of Churchillian rebellion from the Party line were soon in evidence, not least in May 1901 when he spoke out strongly against an increase in the Army Estimates – taking up the issue over which his father had resigned in 1886 – and declaring that re-organization was more important than the expenditure of more money.

Apart from this budget issue, Churchill was equally dismissive about the Secretary of State for War's intention of establishing a standing force of three Army Corps and a reserve of another three Corps, composed of volunteers and Militia, arguing that such a force was both too much and not enough – *'one corps is quite enough to fight savages and three are not enough even to begin to fight Europeans.'* Churchill also believed that it was important to keep up the strength of the Navy, not least because the German Kaiser had begun building up the High Seas Fleet.

In this assessment – which was to be borne out in the coming war – Churchill was again quite correct but, as with his views on their conduct of the South African War, that did not make this speech any more acceptable to the Generals at the War Office. Nor did Churchill's insistence that any spare monies should be spent not on the Army but on the Royal Navy. This, said Churchill, would be money well spent and this view greatly increased Churchill's popularity in nautical circles.

The looming European problem at this time – the threat of a major war – was caused by the rise of Imperial Germany. Following wars with Denmark and Austria, Germany had finally been united under the first Kaiser Wilhelm in 1871, after the Franco-Prussian War in 1870-71. This unity created a powerful industrial state in the heart of the Continent and radically altered the European balance of power. Now, following the dismissal of Chancellor Bismarck, Germany was pursuing an aggressive foreign policy under the third Kaiser, Wilhelm II.

This policy, when added to French *revanchism* over the lost provinces of Alsace and Lorraine, ceded to Germany after 1870, resulted in a European arms race, a search for allies and, most notably for Great Britain, a naval race between Britain and Germany in the building of *Dreadnought* battleships. The end result of all this sabre rattling activity was to set Europe on a course for war.

Long before the issue of a European War became pressing Churchill reached a major point of decision in his political life. Churchill's interests and enthusiasms were clearly on a divergent course from those of the Tory Party, but the issue that brought these matters to a head was that of Free Trade versus Protectionism.

In 1902 Lord Salisbury resigned as Prime Minister. He was replaced by his son-in-law, Arthur Balfour, who appointed a dedicated Free Trader as his Chancellor of the Exchequer. This sowed the seeds for a division that would tear the Conservative Party apart when Balfour's main Party rival, Joseph Chamberlain, endorsed a contrary policy of Protectionism. Divided parties do not win elections and this dispute led to the Tory rout in the elections of 1906.

Churchill was always a devoted Free Trader and when Protectionism became Party policy he was unable to support it. He first declared himself 'an Independent Conservative' and in 1904 he 'crossed the floor of the House' and joined the Opposition, then joining the Liberal Party and standing as the Liberal candidate for North West Manchester in the 1906 elections, in which he was returned with a large majority.

Churchill's 'crossing of the floor of the House' did not meet with widespread approval, even outside the ranks of the Tory Party. It was widely regarded as both disloyal and as an act undertaken to procure some political advantage and to the end of Churchill's life some political figures never forgot this action. Such a step, or so went the accusation, could only be made at the price of his personal integrity – an accusation that became an engrained belief among Churchill's numerous enemies in the House of Commons when he crossed back to the Tory Party later in his career.

Churchill did not see it that way. His argument in 1906 was not that he had left the Party but that the Tory Party had left him – and other Members and much of its *ethos* – by subscribing to policies that the Tories at large could not support. This argument did not attract much favourable comment and there was constant speculation that had Churchill been offered some post in Balfour's Government before 1906 he would have stayed put in the Tory ranks.

This accusation, that Churchill's actions were motivated more by thoughts of personal advantage than by political belief, was bolstered immediately after the election when he was offered the post of Under Secretary to the Colonies. The Secretary of State was Lord Elgin, who sat in the House of Lords, so Churchill became the Government speaker on Colonial matters in the House of Commons, where his former colleagues on the Tory benches gave him a very rough ride.

His first task was to steer a bill through the House covering a new Constitution for what was to become the Union of South Africa. This would give a limited form of self-government to the various republics or provinces, including former colonies like the Cape and Natal but including the Orange Free State and the Transvaal. This bill naturally attracted Churchill's warm support and its passage produced one long-standing and personal benefit.

One of the supporters of this legislation in South Africa was Jan Smuts, an outstanding leader of Boer commandos during the 1901-2 guerrilla war and later Prime Minister of the Union of South Africa – which came into being in 1910. Smuts and Churchill subsequently became lifelong friends; Smuts was one of Churchill's closest advisers and confidants during the Second World War.

Meanwhile, his political career flourishing, Churchill had moved up in the world. In 1908 the Prime Minister, Mr Campbell Bannerman, died and was replaced by Herbert Asquith, formerly the Chancellor of the Exchequer. Asquith's post went to an eloquent Welshman, David Lloyd George, and Churchill became a member of the Cabinet in Lloyd George's former post, President of the Board of Trade. He was just 33 years old and a notable if not especially popular political figure, but his career then suffered a setback. Ministers of the Crown were then obliged to offer themselves to their constituents for re-election and in the resulting Manchester by-election in 1908 Churchill was defeated. Churchill was not out of Parliament for long being quickly elected as Member for Dundee, and fortunately there was a personal compensation for this political reversal: in 1908 he married the beautiful Clementine Hozier.

It had taken the happy couple some time to get to the altar. Churchill met Clementine at a ball in 1904 but they did not get on. Clementine found Churchill gauche and rude as he neither offered to dance with her or take her in to supper and only seemed interested in talking – at length – about himself. Four years later they met again and Churchill proposed in the Temple of Diana at Blenheim where they had been driven to take shelter from a sudden rainstorm. They were married a month later, in September 1908 – David Lloyd George being one of the witnesses – and, as Churchill records, whatever his other vicissitudes, from that moment on he *lived happily ever after.*

Clementine brought some much-needed stability to Churchill's private life and was to prove a shrewd judge of both his friends and his policies. He often took her advice on public matters and was usually wise to do so. Clementine disapproved of his late hours, his heavy drinking, and his gambling and attempted (without any sustained success) to curb their excessive domestic expenditure. This always exceeded their income and led to periodic problems with tradespeople but nothing disabused Churchill of the conviction that income must rise to meet expenditure – curbing the latter to match the former was not an option he thought worth considering. Their life together was not without its problems and dramas but there is no doubt that they loved each other deeply and continued to do so in a long marriage that was to produce five children, of whom four survived.

The post of President of the Board of Trade was largely concerned with routine matters concerned with Britain's principle preoccupation – making money. Anything connected with trade fell within Churchill's remit but as was his custom, he did not let his departmental duties inhibit him from commenting on other Ministers' responsibilities, or sending the PM his views on the issues of the day, of which the most pressing was social reform.

Churchill's interest in social reform – in the welfare of the people – was yet another part of his multifaceted character. His background was aristocratic and Tory but his instincts were liberal and progressive, partly because he saw votes in such policies, but mostly because he thought they were the right ones to follow. In December 1908 he wrote to the Prime Minister laying out not only his views on this issue but also suggesting some practical steps to bring these ideals into being.

There was, said Churchill, tremendous and urgent scope for social welfare policies, and if Germany could establish decent basic conditions for her people why could not Britain, with more assets and a smaller population, do the same? Churchill's letter was not merely rhetoric or exhortation. He listed some practical steps: the establishment of Labour Exchanges to help the unemployed, a National

Infirmity Insurance to help the sick, changes to the Poor Law, and compulsory free state education until the age of seventeen.

In initiating these proposals Churchill establishes a strong claim as a social reformer and his commitment to this aim endured. He soon established the first Labour Exchanges in January 1910, where the out-of-work could find employment. He was vocal in support of Lloyd George's plan for the establishment of old age pensions. He also recruited a young civil servant, William Beveridge, to his staff at the Board of Trade – thirty years later, in 1942, the Beveridge Plan provided the blueprint for Britain's post-war Welfare State. Other steps towards limiting unemployment followed as well as draft legislation establishing unemployment insurance.

These actions fly in the face of one popular perception – that Churchill was always a Tory at heart and that the Tories, by definition, are interested solely in the welfare of the upper classes and capitalism. This point of view is a well-established British myth about the Tories, rather as much of the American public tend to forget that President Lincoln, the great social reformer and the man who abolished slavery in the US, was a Republican, not a Democrat.

Apart from the basic decency that underpins these proposals, there is a merciful absence of cant; Churchill did not pretend that he shared the problems of the poor or had any personal experience of their situation – unlike many modern politicians he did not pretend to 'feel their pain.' He simply felt that such actions were affordable, necessary, and decent.

His motivations, like his solutions, were humanitarian and practical. The condition of the poor was an affront to decency and the decent thing to do was not to spout platitudes, but to do something about it – but if such actions produced electoral benefits, so much the better.

Churchill stayed at the Board of Trade until after the elections of 1910; in the first election he increased his majority in Dundee after which, although hoping for the post of First Lord of the Admiralty, he was offered and accepted the far more important post – at least for an ambitious politician – of Home Secretary, a very senior Cabinet appointment for a man of 35.

The post of Home Secretary is a political minefield – very few Home Secretaries have emerged from that office with increased popularity – but it is a recognised stepping stone on the path to Downing Street. During his time Churchill had to handle three delicate matters – the Suffragettes urging votes for women, the Tonypandy mining strikes, and the Sidney Street siege – but this transfer to the Home Office did not stem his enthusiasm for reform.

Soon after taking office he ordered a review and then a complete overhaul of the prison system which stood in sore need of revision. He introduced a Mines Act aimed at improving both safety and working conditions in the pits. In the former case he did not believe that prison was either a deterrent or of any use whatsoever in criminal reform. One step was to reduce the number of crimes carrying a prison sentence and stem the numbers of young offenders sent to penal institutions which, he felt, offered little more than a further apprenticeship in crime.

One onerous task for the Home Secretary involved taking the final decision in pleas for clemency over death sentences. All such pleas ended up on the Home Secretary's desk and Churchill was only expressing the thoughts of other Home Secretaries in stating that '*This part of the job is beastly.*' Forty-three murderers were sentenced to be hanged during Churchill's time as Home Secretary – a death sentence then being mandatory following a guilty verdict without a jury's plea for clemency – and Churchill exercised his authority to commute half of these to life imprisonment. On the other pleas he wrote the fatal words, '*The law must take its course*' and sent the men to the gallows.

The biggest public order threat at the time came from the Suffragettes, the followers of Mrs Pankhurst pressing for the women's' right to vote. The Home Secretary was a natural target for demonstrations but Churchill saw no benefit in confrontation and urged restraint in both the police response to Suffragette activities – which often led to riots – and in the treatment of Suffragettes in prison, where hunger strikes were their way of carrying on the struggle – and forcible feeding the official response. None of this met with Churchill's approval.

In December 1910 Asquith called another election. Churchill stood in Dundee and was again elected but with a reduced majority. This election came just after Churchill had become involved in the famous Sidney Street Siege, after a group of Latvian anarchists had first staged an armed robbery in which two unarmed policemen were killed and another wounded and then taken shelter in a house in Sidney Street and defied eviction. As Home Secretary, Churchill called for armed military assistance and a platoon of the Scots Guards arrived – though not before the police had attempted to storm the house and suffered another police officer killed and two more wounded. The Guards then took up the battle and in the subsequent exchanges the house caught fire and two anarchists were killed.

This was all very dramatic but the handling of the Sidney Street affair would not have attracted critical comment if Churchill had not gone to the scene himself and – or so it was alleged – attempted to take over the siege and give orders to the Army. The outcome of his appearance in the papers, in a photograph showing the Minister taking cover from bullets, was to fuel a growing belief, held by the Prime Minister and some of the Cabinet, that Churchill was a loose cannon at the Home Office, over-given to dramatic interventions when peaceful negotiation might have been more effective. The fact that there was little evidence to support this belief did not lessen its growth. Further public disquiet over Churchill's character was then caused by the Tonypandy business, a myth with no basis in truth whatsoever but one which was to dog Churchill's reputation in trade union circles for the rest of his life.

Tonypandy is, or was then, a Welsh mining village in the Rhondda valley. Miners were paid on the basis of their output and in November 1910 a dispute arose in the Tonypandy mine over payments for extracting coal from a difficult seam rather than from more productive, easier seams. The strike escalated: the dispute soon came to involve some 20,000 miners in the nearby valleys, with some rioting and the breaking of windows. Feeling unable to control the situation, the Chief Constable of the area police asked the Army's Southern Command for the support of troops.

This would have represented a major escalation in the dispute but fortunately, the General Office Commanding (GOC) Southern Command, Lt-General Neville Macready, was anxious to avoid any confrontation between troops and miners – and was supported in this view by Churchill. Sending in troops to 'Aid the Civil Power,' was a Home Office responsibility and Churchill forbade the troops to move further west than Wiltshire, a hundred miles from the Rhondda. Later, after more rioting, the setting of fires and the one death, he did allow a battalion of the Lancashire Fusiliers into the Rhondda, where they remained, on terms of great amity with the miners, until the end of 1911.

These troops were never used to suppress the miners or intervene in the strike. Riot control was handled throughout the strike by the local police, aided by police reinforcements from London; the most lethal weapon employed by the police in riot control was a rolled-up waterproof cape.

None of this bothered Churchill's detractors, at the time or since. The myth that he *'sent in the troops against the workers'* did not lose anything in the telling and the legend that Tonypandy was the scene of great brutality and the use of naked force by the Army, at Churchill's personal instigation, has never gone away – in spite of all the contrary evidence and the fact that the myth is widely refuted by all directly concerned.

The summer of 1911 saw further strikes, in the docks and railways, but these were overshadowed by the Agadir incident when a German gunboat, the *Panther,* anchored off Agadir, the principal port of Morocco, a country which the French were about to declare a Protectorate. Sending in the *Panther* was seen, correctly, as an act of provocation by the German Kaiser and European political tension went up another notch.

This incident diverted Churchill's mind away from national matters to the wider political scene and, willing as ever to push his ideas forward, within a few days he had produced a plan for the consideration of the Committee of Imperial Defence, outlining a course of action in the event of war – one in which, wrote Churchill – Britain would be allied with France and supported by Russia against a Germany backed by the Austro-Hungarians.

This document, which went so far as to chart the course of this 'war' in the opening weeks, may have been the final straw that convinced Asquith that Churchill must be moved to another position. Within weeks Churchill had been moved to the post he had long wanted – First Lord of the Admiralty – the political head of the British Navy, a post he would occupy until well into the First World War…and one that would bring his career to a seemingly fatal stop.

6. Winston at War

1911-1918

*'Hamilton's Army... had been brought to a standstill
at Gallipoli, was suspended there, was difficult to reinforce
and perilous to withdraw.'*

Winston S. Churchill

Churchill's move from the Home Office to the Admiralty in October 1911 was in some ways a demotion. In peacetime politics at least, being Home Secretary is far more important than being head of the Services and one of the four great offices of State – the others being Foreign Secretary, Chancellor of the Exchequer, and Prime Minister. There is no evidence that Churchill regarded this step as any kind of slight – it was, on the contrary, just the sort of job he enjoyed.

With the Kaiser and Admiral Tirpitz rapidly expanding the German Navy and deepening the Keil Canal so that German warships could slip undetected from the Baltic to the North Sea, there was a big job to be done in preparing the British Navy for a major war – the first it had fought since the Napoleonic Wars in the early 19th century – and Churchill had always expressed a desire for the post.

Churchill's first task at the Admiralty was to create a War Staff, on the lines of the General Staff so recently established at the War Office to consider future strategy and prepare plans for all eventualities. He also needed to establish good relations with Lord Haldane, the currrent Secretary of State for War, partly because it would not do for the two departments of State directly concerned with the security of the realm to be at loggerheads, partly because the plans currently being prepared in secret by the Army General Staff to convey a British Expeditionary Force to France in the event of war with Germany would require the closest co-operation between the Army and the Navy, and such co-operation was not always forthcoming.

There was also a strategic decision that in the event of war the Atlantic would be entrusted to the Royal Navy while the French Fleet occupied itself in the Mediterranean. To this end, Churchill pressed ahead with construction and reform, updating command and control systems, and edging out the current First Sea Lord, the professional head of the Navy, Admiral Sir Arthur Wilson, largely because Wilson was irredeemably opposed to the idea of a Naval Staff. Another major development was the change from coal to oil as the fuel for British warships. This had the effect of making the ships cleaner and faster and far more comfortable for their crews, but increased the dependence on supplies of oil from the ever-volatile Middle East.

Churchill attacked all these issues with his usual vigour and, again as usual, managed to make a number of enemies in the process, but his detractors in the Royal Navy were more than mollified when he managed to increase the Naval Estimates by more than £10 million – his friendship with the Chancellor, Lloyd George played a part here – and did a great deal to improve the pay and conditions for the ordinary seamen and increase the armament of the capital ships. He also succeeded in increasing the number of Dreadnought battleships in the Fleet from the existing twelve to a potential twenty-four, including five of the 'Queen Elizabeth' class with 15-inch guns. Taking everything into account, the sailors were soon more than pleased with their new Ministerial master.

Not that Churchill restricted his activities to the Royal Navy. As usual, he spread himself across the political scene and became closely involved in the hot political issue of the day, Irish Home Rule, a topic that had bedevilled British politics throughout the 19ᵗʰ century and one that was to dominate all other issues until the outbreak of war in August 1914. Given his frequent espousal of policies supported by his father – Lord Randolph was a staunch Unionist who had once produced the phrase *'Ulster will fight and Ulster will be right'* if Home Rule was granted – it is surprising that Churchill now supported Home Rule and was even prepared to speak out in favour of a united Ireland

In taking this public stand and deploring the two other options – continued Westminster rule and Partition – Churchill was flying in the face of political realities. The great majority of the Irish people were Catholic and the Catholics wanted Home Rule – and a United Ireland. The only thing standing in the way was intransigence from the six counties in the Protestant North (Ulster) where Protestants predominated, and they had support for that stand on the mainland, largely from the Tory Party. The Government had to find a way through the twin dilemmas; if they granted independence to a United Catholic Ireland, there would be civil war, but if they opted for Partition and allowed the Northern Protestants a separate state or province, they would lay the groundwork for endless division among the Irish people.

The final option, to maintain the *status quo* and rule Ireland from Westminster, was no longer viable but the issue required careful handling and a great amount of tact – something Churchill was not always good at supplying. In this case his urging that the Unionist should think of Ireland as a whole and not of their own sectarian interests was both sensible and doomed. His speeches on Home Rule met with a hostile response in Ulster and failed to change any opinions on this most enduring issue.

Irish matters continued to simmer until the Spring of 1914, distracting politicians from the situation on the Continent. Matters came to a head with the 'Curragh Incident' that Easter, when a number of Army officers stationed at the Curragh outside Dublin resigned their commissions in protest against rumours that their unit, the 3rd Cavalry Brigade, was to be ordered into Ulster to coerce the Protestants into a United Ireland. At the same time Churchill ordered a cruiser squadron to the take station off the North Irish coast and patrol Belfast Lough – an action to which the Protestants took great exception. Carson, the Protestant leader, was openly urging the Protestants to take up arms – and importing rifles and ammunition for the purpose – and the 3rd Cavalry officers enjoyed widespread support when they declared that it was no part of their duty to drive British citizens into the arms of another State. Civil war seemed all too probable when news arrived from the Balkans.

The final outcome of this continuing dispute in 1914 was both Home Rule for Ireland and Partition – both of which were deferred until the end of the First World War, which Britain entered, after some hesitation on 4 August, 1914.

When the First World War broke out that summer Britain had the largest navy in the World and the political master of that navy – the First Lord of the Admiralty – was Winston Churchill. The simmering tension in Continental Europe had been coming to the boil for weeks, ever since the assassination of the Austrian heir, the Archduke Franz-Ferdinand in Sarajevo at the end of June. Alliances were invoked, threats issued, armies mobilised, and on 1 August, these Continental armies – Russian, German, French, Austro-Hungarian, and Serbian – began to march.

Churchill did not wait for Britain's declaration of war on 4 August. This declaration was motivated by the German invasion of neutral Belgium – a country whose neutrality had been guaranteed by a number of European nations, including Britain and Germany, as long ago as 1839. On a less altruistic note the British Government, and Churchill in particular, saw the need to prevent Germany establishing naval bases on the North Sea and Channel coast – both issues doing rather more to make the British take up arms than any particular desire to aid the French.

When the European armies began to mobilise, Churchill promptly ordered the Fleet to its war stations and supported Asquith in his decision to declare war on Germany and send the British Expeditionary Force to France. The pre-war arrangements to ship the BEF overseas went like clockwork; within days, British infantry, artillery and cavalry were pouring ashore at the French Channel ports and marching hard for the Belgian frontier; not one man was lost on the way over.

The Royal Navy had succeeded in its first task and was soon blockading the German coast, but all did not go well in the first months of the war. A contest between Britain and Germany has been described as one between a whale and an elephant, the one powerful at sea, the other mighty on land. At first the German elephant carried all before it; the French forces and the BEF were driven back from the Belgian frontier to the Marne before the successful counter-attack in September. In the following weeks and months the 'Race to the Sea', the flanking marches of the opposing armies north and west from the river Aisne to the Channel coast, and digging in when they met, saw the establishment of trench lines along the Western Front. This 1914 trench position became the Old Front Line, a 400-mile long scar over which the European armies would waste themselves for the next four years – by December 1914 the land war in Europe was a stalemate and the British and French Cabinets and Staff were seeking some way to break the deadlock.

Nor were matters going better at sea. Churchill's first setback was the escape of the German warships *Goeben* and *Breslau*, which evaded the Mediterranean Fleet and reached Constantinople. This provided Germany with a propaganda coup, for Britain had been constructing a battleship for the Turkish Navy and when war broke out Turkish sailors were already in the UK, ready to man this ship and sail it home. The British decided that such a powerful naval unit could not be given up and, much to the fury of the Turkish Government, refused to hand it over. Germany therefore stepped into the dispute and ordered the *Goeben* and *Breslau* transferred to the Turkish Navy. This event was a humiliation for Churchill and the Royal Navy and a step that took Turkey into the war on the side of Germany on 1 November, 1914.

Worse was to follow. In September three British cruisers were sunk in an hour by a German submarine and more than 1,000 British sailors were lost. In November a German squadron destroyed the British South American Squadron at the Battle of Coronel off the coast of Chile, a disaster barely matched by the destruction of the German ships a few weeks later in the Battle of the Falkland Islands when four German ships were sunk. This triumph was overshadowed by the bombardment of British coastal towns by German warships, an action the Royal Navy failed to prevent.

Nor was this all. While success continued to elude him at sea, Churchill had problems at the Admiralty. On the outbreak of war, rampant xenophobia had gripped the British public; German shops were wrecked, German restaurants boycotted, even dachshunds and German Shepherd dogs became unpopular. Public anger, fuelled by these naval reverses, began to concentrate on the First Sea Lord, Admiral Prince Louis of Battenberg, an officer of German descent but impeccable loyalty.

In spite of Churchill's open support, Prince Louis was eventually forced to resign, leaving office in November 1914. Prince Louis changed his family name to Mountbatten even as the Royal Family abandoned the name Saxe-Coborg-Gotha for that of the House of Windsor. Prince Louis was the father or Lord Louis Mountbatten, who became a prominent figure in the Second World War, and this combination was completed in 1947 when Prince Louis's great-nephew, Philip Mountbatten, married Princess Elizabeth, granddaughter of King George V, and later Queen Elizabeth II.

Churchill replaced Prince Louis with a retired Admiral, Lord Fisher, now aged 73, a former First Sea Lord who had brought the Royal Navy into the Dreadnought era and was highly regarded in the naval service. This move was not inspired. Fisher was an autocrat and not given to following orders. He had little time for his young political master and a very large ego; before long the two men were on a collision course.

Given the problems facing him, Churchill might have been well advised to stay in the Admiralty and address these difficulties with all the time and talent as his disposal but that, as ever, was not Churchill's way. He was soon taking an interest in other aspects of the war, and seeking closer action with the enemy.

In October 1914 Churchill became directly involved in an ill-fated attempts to save the Belgian port of Antwerp from falling into German hands. He first sent a 2000-strong Royal Marine Brigade to reinforce the Belgian garrison and then went over himself, helping to organise the defence and sending cables to London, suggesting to the Cabinet that he leave the Admiralty, be appointed to the rank of Lt-General, and remain in Antwerp and lead the Anglo-Belgian forces. The Cabinet greeted this offer with some hilarity. Churchill was ordered home to handle his appointed duties and leave the battle in France and Belgium to the soldiers. General Rawlinson was entrusted with the defence of Antwerp, which held out until the end of November.

Churchill's chronic desire for action and adventure are again on display at this time, but there was another side to these activities. While in Antwerp Churchill had ordered the construction of armoured cars – basically Rolls-Royce cars covered with steel plates. These were armed with machine guns and sent out to scour the countryside, harass the enemy and pick up any shot-down British airmen from the Royal Flying Corps. This task was accomplished successfully but revealed one snag; these 'armoured cars' were road-bound. What was needed was a vehicle that could operate off roads and such a vehicle, the prototype of the tank, was even then being contemplated by more active minds in Britain.

The 'tank' – the name arose when, for security reasons, the shrouded shapes of these armoured fighting vehicles were described as water-tanks – was constructed rather than invented, as the basic ingredients of tracks, internal combustion engine, and armoured plate already existed.

The higher minds interested in developing a tracked armoured vehicle got no support or funds from the Army but were able to engage the attention of the First Lord. Taking a somewhat flexible approach to the problem, Churchill decided that these 'landships' had potential for the war then developing on the Western Front where some means had to be found to overcome the obstacle presented to the attacker by the combination of muddy ground, barbed wire, machine-guns and artillery. Churchill decided to provide the funds for development and the early trials.

By the end of 1915 these Admiralty-sponsored 'landships' had become the first tanks. When they first lumbered into action at the Battle of Flers-Courcelette in September 1916, they introduced a new and decisive weapon to the battlefield. Winston Churchill, if not the 'Father of the Tank,' can with some reason be regarded as the midwife; without his assistance the tank would have taken much longer to arrive.

Developing the tank took time. Meanwhile losses mounted to the millions, attack after attack led only to higher losses, and the politicians and generals, French and British, all sought some way of moving this war away from the Western Front and outflanking the enemy in some other theatre. At the end of December 1914, Churchill sent a detailed letter to Prime Minister Asquith, suggesting that there were two ways of getting around the defences of the Western Front.

Churchill had seen the effect of modern weapons in South Africa and shied away from the inevitable slaughter that a campaign on the Western Front would inevitably involve. He was, in the jargon of the time, an Easterner, someone who believed that – since they were simply too strong to be breached by direct attack– the German defences on the Western Front must be outflanked, and there were only two places which offered the necessary opportunity.

The first was to make a major amphibious landing on the coast of Schleswig-Holstein, south of Denmark. If successful, this landing would close the Kiel Canal to German warships and enable neutral Denmark to join the war. There was no sign that Denmark was eager to do this but if the Danes could be so persuaded, the British and French could soon have an Army within a hundred miles of Berlin.

The second alternative, Churchill declared, lay at the eastern end of the Mediterranean by forcing the passage of the Dardanelles, taking Constantinople and so driving Turkey out of the war – and with any luck bringing Greece and other Balkan states into the war on the side of the Entente. This last proposal led to the disastrous Gallipoli campaign with which Churchill's name has always been connected, one that was to blight his reputation in the decades up to 1940.

The aims of the Gallipoli campaign were simple and, had they been achieved, beneficial. A success in the Dardanelles would have provided a (somewhat circuitous) way around the stalemate of the Western Front and drive Turkey out of the war. This last was the most obvious benefit because it would thereby remove the growing Turkish threat to both the Suez Canal and the Persian oilfields, both so vital to the Royal Navy. It would also open up a supply route to Russia and so increase the pressure on Germany's eastern front. All these were desirable aims but the plan to achieve them was flawed in concept and hesitant in execution. Moreover, the plan was Churchill's and the initial execution in the hands of the Royal Navy. When it all went wrong, Churchill had to take the blame.

Although the bibliography on the Gallipoli campaign is massive and often controversial, the bulk of the evidence suggests that the naval and military leaders of the day had neither the kit nor the competence for a major amphibious operation of the kind that breaching the Dardanelles defences must entail. Not that an amphibious operation was contemplated, at least initially, when the operation was proposed in the New Year of 1915.

The Belgian forts had been destroyed by heavy artillery and it seemed likely that the Dardanelles defences could be destroyed in much the same fashion by naval gunfire and allow the Fleet through to overawe Constantinople. This was the first of many mistakes – the notion that the Royal Navy could force the Straits and win the battle without the aid of ground forces. This was Churchill's belief and led to the latest of his increasingly frequent disputes with Admiral Fisher.

To achieve this purpose Churchill had one advantage, a number of slow but heavily armed battleships that were no longer viable for Fleet operations against faster ships, but would do very well as gun platforms for shore bombardments. These ships were duly brought to the Eastern Mediterranean and deployed to force the Dardanelles straits. This took time, and British intentions were known to the Turks before the Royal Navy attacked for the first time on 18 March, 1915 – and the result was disaster.

The Turkish shore batteries gave back shot for shell and, although they did not kill many French or British seamen, they knocked these old warships about a bit and encouraged the captains to close the range in order to finish the job quickly. This lured the ships into carefully laid and ill-swept Turkish minefields. Two battleships were lost with considerable loss of life and the combined French and British Fleets withdrew to lick their wounds. This reverse produced another row between the First Lord and Admiral Fisher, when the latter was reluctantly obliged to send a signal to Admiral de Robeck, the commander at the Dardanelles, ordering another attack.

Admiral de Robeck declined to induce another disaster and the Dardanelles campaign became an Army matter following an amphibious assault on April 25, after a force of British, French, Gurkha, Australian and New Zealand troops under Churchill's old friend, General Sir Ian Hamilton, was mustered in the Aegean and Egypt and sent ashore in April 1915 – and was held on the beach with great loss. Thus began the notorious Gallipoli campaign, which went on until the end of 1915 and cost a great quantity of lives before the troops were withdrawn in the early days of 1916.

The Gallipoli campaign opened up all the half-hidden rifts between Churchill and Fisher but the root of the Gallipoli debacle was a lack of knowledge in both naval and military circles of the principles and inherent snags of amphibious operations. This was hardly surprising; Britain had not engaged in a European war for almost 100 years and even the Napoleonic Wars, while active at sea, had seen little landing of troops on hostile shores. Even if there had been an amphibious tradition in Britain, increases in the scale of military operations and the development of technology would have made many historic lessons and techniques out of date.

All that said there were other failures that cannot be overlooked. For example, when the admiral off Gallipoli was asked how long it would take the naval task force to reduce the Turkish forts guarding the Dardenelles, he replied that a month should do it. Quite apart from the loss of surprise, an essential military asset, this month long bombardment must surely have tipped the Turks' hand to British intentions – and one might ask what the Turks would be doing while their forts were steadily reduced – except constructing a further defence line beyond the range of naval gunfire.

Churchill was blamed for this debacle and while the failures in command during the landings and in the subsequent fighting are hardly his fault, he cannot escape criticism for his insistence that the Royal Navy could carry the Straits alone – a conviction which tipped the Turks to the entire operation and fatally undermined every subsequent attempt to retrieve the position. Surprise was vital and once that was lost, nothing could be achieved. Day by day the Turkish positions grew stronger and the outcome inevitably unfavourable to the landing force.

Whatever damage the Gallipoli fiasco did to Churchill's later reputation, it simply confounded the other problems he brought on himself by either unwise comments and letters to Asquith, or unwarranted interference with other departments. By the time Gallipoli was seen as a disaster, Churchill had run out of friends in Government and in Parliament. Perhaps the strain of the Gallipoli campaign was proving too much, but in May and June Churchill managed to quarrel with Kitchener, Lloyd George and Asquith, usually over matters that were outside Churchill's remit.

All this alienated Cabinet support and did nothing for his personal popularity; his position was not helped in May 1915 when his professional colleague, Admiral Fisher, resigned from his post and refused to return. Another more serious and wider scandal augmented the subsequent outcry over this defection: the so-called 'shell shortage' on the Western Front, recently revealed at the battles of Neuve Chapelle and Aubers Ridge.

These attacks had cost the BEF some 20,000 men without a yard of territorial gain and Field Marshal Sir John French had placed the blame for this on his inability to support the infantry with artillery – since the guns had run out of ammunition. The outcome was a political crisis leading to the formation of a Coalition government. The Tory leader, Andrew Bonar Law, flatly declined to lead his party into Government with the Liberals while Churchill, the defector from Tory ranks and the instigator of the Gallipoli fiasco, remained at the Admiralty. Churchill had meanwhile reformed his Board of Admiralty with Sir Arthur Wilson back as First Sea Lord, but Asquith, knowing that the Tories were after Churchill's scalp, refused to accept these changes. It was now clear to all that there was no place for Churchill in a coalition Government.

Asquith did not like this but he had no option; Churchill, protesting wildly, was obliged to resign from the Admiralty – the post of First Lord going to Arthur Balfour – and given the sinecure post of Chancellor of the Duchy of Lancaster. From commanding the mightiest navy in the world, he was now obliged to occupy himself with minor issues and home affairs. Nor was this all; further demotion followed. For a short while he remained on what was known as the Dardanelles Committee but when this was reformed and renamed the War Cabinet, he was excluded from membership.

One long-term benefit arose during this time. Churchill was spending a weekend at the country house of his sister-in-law, brother Jack's wife, Lady Gwendolyn, and came upon the lady painting in the garden. Churchill took a look at her work and was urged to have a go himself, which he did with considerable enjoyment and not a little skill. Watercolours soon gave way to oils, his skill developed and, over time, Churchill became an extremely competent landscape artist.

Whether his paintings would have commanded a market, and a respectable price, had it not been for his political reputation is hard to say, but his paintings are much more than mere daubs and would not disgrace any collector's wall or public gallery. More to the point, though, was painting's role in Churchill's life, as a distraction from constant work and a way out of his periodic fits of deep depression – the '*black dog*' as he called it, which was to appear in later life.

Painting was certainly a solace now; Churchill was only forty but it appeared that his career was over. This being so, in November 1915, Churchill resigned from the Government – though retaining his Parliamentary seat – and rejoined the Army, volunteering for service on the Western Front.

As with his other military adventures, Churchill's time on active service was brief. Although only a Major in the Oxfordshire Hussars – a Yeomanry regiment – he dined with Sir John French on his first night in France and began to lobby for a brigade command, which would have carried the rank of one-star general.

This struck everyone as a somewhat rapid promotion for an officer whose previous military career had peaked at full lieutenant in a cavalry regiment twelve years before, and it was suggested that he might first acquaint himself with front line conditions by spending some time with the 2nd Battalion, The Grenadier Guards, and then, on promotion to Lieutenant-Colonel, begin with the command of a battalion.

Churchill spent 12 days with the Grenadiers and did well; he might have stayed with them but he still hankered after a brigade – even writing to Clementine asking her to order him a brigadier's tunic before Sir John French, who might have given in on this point, was sacked following the disasters at Loos in September and replaced by General Sir Douglas Haig, an altogether sterner character who had no intention whatsoever of placing a brigade in Churchill's willing but inexperienced hands. On New Year's Day, 1916 Churchill was given command of the 6th Battalion, The Royal Scots Fusiliers, which was reforming after taking heavy casualties at Loos.

Somewhat to everyone's surprise – except, of course, his own – Churchill did well with his new command, rapidly raising morale and efficiency before taking the battalion into the trenches at the end of January. They took up a position near the village of Ploegsteert – Plugstreet to the Jocks – where they stayed for the next five weeks, alternating between the front line and the reserve trenches.

Although no major offensive was in hand, this time was not without danger. Churchill wrote to Clementine that two of the five officers at battalion HQ had been hit in the first week – recording at the same time how frustrating it was to be in France, away from the centres of power in London and how anxious he was to return. Clementine, though worried over his safety, still felt that it was too soon for him to return to Parliament and public life and advised him to stay with the battalion. *'Wait, wait, have patience. Your motive for going to the Front was easily understood,'* she wrote in early April 1916, *'your motive for coming back requires explanation.'*

Patience was not a Churchillian virtue, and the Gallipoli issue had not been resolved by the recent evacuation of the peninsula. He therefore took some leave and took part in a debate in the House in which, to general amazement, he urged Balfour to recall Fisher to the post of First Sea Lord.

Churchill was not in the House to hear the comments of another naval officer, Admiral Sir Hedworth Meux – a savage reply to Chuchill's proposals which concluded *'I am sorry the late First Lord is not in his place – We all wish him well in France and hope he will stay there,'* but he was present when Balfour rose to deliver a crushing reply to Churchill's suggestion:

> *'My right honourable friend has often astonished the House but I do not think he ever astonished it so much as when he came down to explain that the remedy for all our ills as far as the Navy is concerned is to get rid of Sir Henry Jackson and put in his place Lord Fisher.*
>
> *I cannot follow the workings of the right honourable gentleman's mind. He told the Prime Minister when Prince Louis resigned that the only man he could work with was Lord Fisher. Is it not extraordinary*

that the only man with whom my right honourable friend could consent to work at the Admiralty was the most distinguished sailor who after five months, refused to work with my right honourable friend.'

Churchill could make no effective reply to this ironic masterpiece and retired in some disorder, but his return to France was brief, for in early May it was decided that the two depleted battalions, the 6th and 7th Royal Scots Fusiliers, should be amalgamated – and since the colonel of the 7th Battalion was senior to Churchill, he was given the command. This suited Churchill admirably and on 7 May he returned to London and resumed his political career.

Parliament was in turmoil, not least because of the recent events in Ireland where the Easter Rebellion had just taken place in Dublin, a desperate and unpopular move by a group of Republicans unwilling to wait until the war was over to achieve their promised independence. The rebellion had not lasted long and the rebels received a hostile reception from the Irish population when they emerged from their positions and were marched away. This unpopularity changed to sympathy and anger when the British Government, quite properly but most unwisely, tried the rebels for treason and had several of them shot – so providing the Republican cause with fresh martyrs for the good old cause.

Nor was this all. The long awaited combined offensive on the Somme was due to open in June – it finally began on 1 July – and the necessary introduction of conscription, never before employed in Britain, was another source of public disquiet. Churchill flung himself into the debate on all these topics and was given a reception that varied from the interested to the dismissive, the latter with frequent references to the Dardanelles.

He made a more effective intervention following the drawn naval battle of Jutland on 1 June: the British lost more ships and men but the German High Seas Fleet retired from the scene and never left port again. Hopes of a return to office rose with the death of Kitchener, drowned in June while en route to Russia, but when the Cabinet was restructured it was Lloyd George who got the post of Secretary of State for War, and Churchill failed in his aim of occupying Lloyd George's old post at the Ministry of Munitions.

Lacking more work to fill his time he turned again to journalism, writing a series of articles for the *Sunday Pictorial* – a journal less prestigious but more profitable than the *Daily Telegraph*, while preparing for his long hoped-for appearance before the Dardanelles Commission of Enquiry where he intended to vindicate his actions and decisions of the previous year. In the event the Commission sat in camera, so Churchill, though giving evidence, had no opportunity to introduce legal counsel or cross-examine other witnesses.

Meanwhile the battle of the Somme ground its bloody path across Picardy, killing thousands of men every day for no appreciable territorial gain. That battle ended in early December and was soon overshadowed, at least in political circles, by the fall of Asquith and the appointment of Lloyd George as Prime Minister of the Coalition Government. Given their long association and apparent friendship, Churchill not unnaturally assumed that the new PM would have work for him – but it was not to be, or not yet. Churchill was still unpopular among Liberals and unwanted by the Conservatives. It was not until July 1917, eight months after entering Downing Street, that Lloyd George offered Churchill the post of Minister of Munitions – a post which he occupied with his usual vigor until the Great War ended in November 1918.

7. In and Out of Office

1919 - 1939

*'History best remembers Churchill
in the 1930's – his Wilderness Years.'*

Roy Jenkins

The inter-war years, those two disturbed decades between the end of the First World War and the outbreak of the Second were a time of mixed fortune for Winston Churchill. His political career faltered, in the sense that he was usually out of office, but he was not out of the political spotlight and his warning voice was eventually heard, though barely in time to avoid catastrophe.

During the difficult post-war period, up to the Wall Street Crash of 1929 and especially after the rise of Fascism from when Hitler came to power in 1933, Churchill's views, and Churchill's voice, was increasingly heard and gradually listened to. Curiously enough, it was at this time, when he had no official position, that the ground was prepared for his final rise to power in 1940.

This period began well. At the end of 1918 he was offered the choice of returning to his old post at the Admiralty or taking on wider tasks at the War Office – a post that would include responsibility for the nascent Royal Air Force. There was first an election – the Khaki Election of 1919, which returned both Churchill and Lloyd George's coalition Government. This election also marked the final downfall of the Liberal Party – well over two-thirds of the returned MPs were Conservatives and the rag-tag opposition consisted of Socialists (Labour), Sinn Feiners from Southern Ireland (who refused to take their Westminster seats and were awaiting the long promised Irish Free State), what was left of the Liberals and a band of Ulster Unionists and some Independent Conservatives – who declined to serve with either Lloyd George or Churchill.

In the immediate post-war period Lloyd George was mainly concerned with the Paris Peace Talks, that series of conferences that attempted to heal the wounds and punish the guilty of the First World War – and succeeded in playing a major part in creating the situation that led inexorably to the Second World War. Churchill meanwhile went to the War Office, back in power again aged only 44, and worked in Lloyd George's absence with Bonar Law, who led the coalition Conservatives until his replacement by Austen Chamberlain in 1921 – only for Chamberlain and Lloyd George to fall from office in 1922.

Churchill's first task was demobilisation, the return to civilian life – and unemployment – of three million British soldiers. His other task, to which he devoted considerable enthusiasm, was to encourage any efforts to counter the establishment of the Bolsheviks in Russia and the spread of Communism elsewhere – to this end there was an Allied force of some 30,000 men in Russia, half of them British, a scanty force with which to counter Trotsky's Red Army.

From the outbreak of the Russian Revolution in 1917, Churchill regarded the advent of Communist power in Russia as an unmitigated evil. Had he been empowered to do so, he would have been eager to plot the Soviet downfall. *'The strangling of Bolshevism at its birth would have been a blessing to the human race'* he said 30 years later, but he could get no support for intervention and the British forces were withdrawn.

During this period he suffered some considerable personal grief, the first coming in June 1921 when his mother, Lady Jennie, died following a fall; the second came two months later in August, when his youngest daughter, Marigold, died of diphtheria. All in all, both personally and professionally, the years from 1919 to 1922 were not a happy time.

His parallel career, as an historian and writer continued to flourish. Churchill was now working on another major work, *The World Crisis,* a multi-volume history of the Great War – which was found, when published, to consist largely of personal views and reminiscences. He continued to live life at full bore, travelling continuously, entertaining lavishly, and drinking more than somewhat in spite of those periodic cash crises, which were never to go away until the years after the Second World War.

Nor was the world peaceful. There were problems in the Levant, between the Greeks and the Turks, and Churchill soon became involved in lengthy, complicated, and not always successful negotiations with the French over Syria, with the Jews and Arabs over Palestine following the Balfour Declaration which supported the notion of a homeland for the Jews, and with the Iraqis over Mesopotamia and the Persian Gulf oil fields. As ever unable to keep his fingers out of other peoples' pies, he was also vocal on the Irish question and became involved in the negotiations over the establishment of the Irish Free State in 1921.

In the following year Churchill's domestic arrangements, which had so far involved transferring his family from one large but rented property to another, finally achieved a more stable base with his purchase of a country house – Chartwell in Kent, a county Churchill had learned to love at the knee of his nanny, Mrs Everest. Chartwell, a red-brick house in extensive gardens, had Elizabethan roots but was largely Victorian. Although large enough for his family, the necessary staff and a constant stream of visitors, was not at all grand.

On the other hand Chartwell was less than an hour from London by car (in those traffic-free days, at least) and he could afford it. The purchase price was just £5,000 – say $250,000 in modern money – and although a similar sum had to be spent on repairs and redecoration before the family could move in in 1924, it became Churchill's country home, his place of refuge in the hard and troublesome years ahead.

Later on, during his 'wilderness years' in the 1930s, Churchill took a direct hand in the work of improving Chartwell, notably by building walls. Wall building is a skilled trade; get it wrong and the wall can collapse, with dire results for anyone standing underneath. This thought clearly did not bother Churchill, who never let his total ignorance of any matter prevent his participation. He found bricklaying absorbing and highly therapeutic and his walls were not small, insignificant, knee-high structures but imposing works, some well over head height – and still standing today, decades after Churchill's death.

In the early 1920's Churchill became caught up in the Chanak Incident, one of the many problems arising from the decisions taken at the various Paris Peace Conferences of 1919-20. The Allied Treaty with the Turks, the Paris Treaty of Sevres, had inflicted penalties on Turkey for supporting Germany in the war and handed long stretches of the Turkish coast to Greece. The Turks, under their new leader Ataturk – Mustapha Kemal – resisted this move strongly and turned to arms. An army under Ataturk chased the Greek garrisons away from the Turkish coast and threatened to cross the Dardanelles at Chanak, where their path was barred by a small British force.

This incident caused considerable alarm in London. When the Cabinet considered the Turkish action tantamount to war, Churchill ordered up more troops and asked the Dominion Governments for troops, leaking this plea to the newspapers as a way of putting pressure on the Dominion Prime Ministers. They were not amused. The British commander at Chanak managed to dissuade the Turks from further advances and the affair petered out – but did no good to Churchill's still-fragile Ministerial reputation. He was increasingly seen around

Westminster as a loose cannon, a belligerent politician - and an unsuccessful minister.

The Chanak Incident, and Churchill's part in fomenting it, brought down the fragile Liberal-Tory coalition that had endured since 1916. The Conservative Party members were tired of being tied to Lloyd George's Liberal coat tails. In October 1922, they threw over their leader Austen Chamberlain and elected a new leader, Bonar Law. This action led to another General Election in which Churchill lost his seat. For Lloyd George the situation was even more serious; after a steady ascent to power since 1900 he was out of Government and never held office again.

It took Churchill two years to get back into Parliament and in the process he again cruised across the political spectrum. He contested two by-elections, the first as a Liberal. He stood for the second by-election as an 'Independent Anti-Socialist.' He took this stance, so abandoning the Liberal whip, partly because the Liberals had formed a coalition with Labour in the hung Parliament of 1923, but specifically over the issue of recognizing Soviet Russia, an action to which the Socialists were firmly committed and Churchill resolutely opposed.

Once again his principles were at odds with his Party – so once again he crossed the floor of the House of Commons. This action took a little time. Churchill was not welcome in the Tory ranks, and in the third General Election of this unsteady period between 1922-24 Churchill stood for the Epping constituency as a 'Constitutionalist' candidate. With the support of the local Conservative Party, who declined to oppose him, he got home easily in a general Conservative landslide.

This election of 1924 marked the end of the Liberal Party as a political force; its fortunes did not begin to revive until the end of the century and then only in conjunction with dissident Socialists – the Social Democrats - to form the Liberal Democratic Party of today.

Meantime Churchill was continuing with this literary career. He occupied much of the time between 1922-24 in writing his history of the First World War *The World Crisis*. Although this book covers all the events of World War I it is, in the main, an explanation of Churchill's actions and a generally successful attempt to spread the blame for those actions – notably the Dardanelles – for which he had been held largely responsible. Arthur Balfour remarked caustically but accurately that, *'Winston has written a book about himself and called it The World Crisis,'* but criticism of Churchill's views did not prevent the book selling well and making him a useful amount of money – money continuing to drain from his pockets steadily at this time.

After the General Election of 1924, Stanley Baldwin became Prime Minister. Churchill was not only accepted back into the Tory fold, he was offered a senior post in the Cabinet – but unfortunately that of Chancellor of the Exchequer, a most unsuitable appointment for someone of Churchill's experience and inclinations. Churchill had no knowledge of economics and no great interest in learning, yet he was plunged almost at once into a highly complicated monetary issue: whether Britain should return to the gold standard at the pre-war dollar sterling rate of £1=\$4.86. Even Churchill doubted whether Britain's worn-out industry and empty Treasury could sustain such a rate and he was warned of the dire effect this would have on exports and employment by no less an expert than John Maynard Keynes. However, the City and the capitalists were all in favour of a return to the Gold Standard and Churchill gave way, with inevitable results.

Unemployment promptly soared; exports fell, and in 1926 came a crippling strike in the mining industry followed by a General Strike, which damaged the country's economic condition still further and left industry and nation poorly prepared for the slump that followed the crash of 1929. On top of the allegations over Tonypandy earlier in the century, the breaking of the 1926 General Strike made Churchill a reviled figure to the British working class.

Churchill remained Chancellor of the Exchequer until the Tory Government fell in 1929. This was followed, briefly, by the Labour (Socialist) Government of Ramsay MacDonald but MacDonald was equally unable to solve the nation's economic woes and a National Government, dominated by the Tories but led by Ramsay MacDonald, was created in 1931. MacDonald remained Prime Minister until 1935 when he was replaced by Stanley Baldwin, but neither Prime Minister had a place in his Cabinet for Winston Churchill.

The 1930s are described in most Churchill histories as Winston's 'Wilderness Years' – out of office and out of favour. Much of this on-going disapproval stemmed from Churchill's engrained opposition to any form of self-government for India, a vast sub-continent then moving inexorably towards Dominion status, the penultimate step before full independence. In taking this stand over India Churchill was flying in the face of every party in Parliament including all but a few rampant imperialists in the Conservative Party. He was also defying the logic of the Empire's political process for the old Dominions – Australia, New Zealand, Canada, South Africa – had already broken away and it was certain that India would follow – and equally certain that attempts to restrict this happening would lead to trouble in Britain and in India.

Like any politician with claims to the title of statesman, Churchill had vision but on this issue his vision was clouded by the fact, or at any rate by the belief, that if India went the rest of the British Empire would follow, with dire subsequent consequences for Britain and the world. This belief can be traced to the fact that Churchill held, and would continue to hold, the unfashionable view that the British Empire was a force for good and stability in a dangerous world and that chaos would follow its fall. Events have since proved that Churchill was absolutely right but the tide of history was flowing against him.

Standing in the path of Indian independence did Churchill no good and his constant harping on the Indian issue wore out the patience of his supporters and gave comfort to his numerous enemies. Several years were wasted in this fashion but they were also years of incessant activity, certainly after 1933 when Adolph Hitler came to power in Germany. The Nazis began their march towards the domination and subjugation of Europe, and the British Government began a process of 'appeasement,' hoping to placate Hitler by meeting any of his demands that could be seen as reasonable – most often those arising from the flawed Treaty of Versailles.

The flaws in the Versailles Treaty are too numerous to list here, but several of the clauses provided Germany with a legitimate sense of grievance which Hitler and the Nazi Party were able to exploit later. The first was the matter of reparations, money paid out, largely to France, to compensate for the damage caused to France during the First World War. Some reparation payment was clearly justified but the sum for reparations was set far too high and well above Germany's ability to pay. The German economy, gravely damaged in the war, could not stand the strain of large reparations, and soon collapsed; in 1923 the German mark was valued at *four million* to one US dollar.

The second German grievance was over self-determination. This was a particular project of US President Woodrow Wilson, who wanted every European nation to have its own nation-state, largely composed of its own nationals. The only exception to this rule was the Austrians, who were not allowed to join with the Germans as they wished to do.

Germany also felt herself unduly penalised in all the peace negotiations where the terms demanded by the Entente Powers – the US, France, Britain and Italy – went beyond those laid out in the Fourteen Points on which Germany had agreed to the armistice, and by the 'war guilt' clause in the Versailles Treaty which obliged Germany to admit to all the blame for the outbreak of war in the first place.

Apart from these specifically German problems, Germany formed part of a Continent where the liberal political consensus was under attack from Left and Right. The threat from the Left – Communism – was the lesser one as the Bolsheviks were fully absorbed at this time in tightening their grip on Russia, eliminating the Mensheviks and murdering the *kulaks* – the more prosperous peasants. This left the rest of Europe as the prey of the Right.

Between the two World Wars there were 28 separate nation-states in Europe. By 1920 all but two of these were democracies – at least in the sense that they had elected Parliaments, a range of political parties, and some form of liberal constitution. By 1939 no fewer than 16 of these had become dictatorships, mostly of the Right, and in the following year seven of these were over-run by the Germans or Italians. By the summer of 1940 there were only five democracies left in Europe. Three of these – Switzerland, Ireland, and Sweden – were neutral and Finland was reluctantly allied to Germany. Of the original 28, by the end of 1940, only Great Britain stood against the Fascist powers. Much of the credit for that must go to Winston Churchill.

The collapse of democratic Europe in the 1920's largely arose from economic factors; it was perceived that liberal governments and liberal constitutions were not adequate for times of great economic hardship. Too much time was spent arguing and compromising when what was needed was the smack of firm government and some decisive action – this at least was the message of the Right, who found a ready scapegoat in the Liberals and the Left and an attentive audience among the millions of unemployed – and plenty of recruits for their street war with the other contender for power- the Communists and Marxists.

Slowly, but with increasing speed, the Right took over. Benito Mussolini, the prototype Fascist dictator, took over in Italy in October 1922. Over the next decade the Weimar Republic collapsed in Germany, democracy came under threat everywhere, and the remaining democracies attempted to cope with the situation by compromise and debate.

Churchill was the exception to this generality. Out of power from the election of May 1929, he was now more mature and less volatile than ten years before. He took this defeat calmly, refrained from seeking another post and turned instead to his other career – writing. He completed work on *The World Crisis* and started on an entertaining biography, *My Early Life,* which was published in 1930 and did very well, being translated into a number of languages and eventually in 1960 becoming a motion picture.

In producing this work, in such a short time and amid his other preoccupations, reveals that Churchill was already a fluent writer, able to produce accurate well-written copy without the need for lengthy time-consuming rewrites. *My Early Life* is a delightful book, exciting and humorous, enjoyable to read and very probably enjoyable to write.

He also travelled, renewing his acquaintance with the US and Canada after a considerable gap, making speeches, meeting old friends and new ones and making a considerable amount of money, writing to Clementine in September that his book work and journalism had brought in the tidy sum of over £20,000, and with careful investment should set them up for life.

Much of this money came from the advance for a major work, the life of his distinguished ancestor, John Churchill, First Duke of Marlborough. Completing this book *Marlborough* took up a great deal of his time over the next few years, but his other main activity, journalism, was largely concerned with alerting Government, Parliament, and public to the growing menace of Fascism – and from 1933, the rise of Nazi Germany under Adolph Hitler. Journalism was necessary; the illusion that he was comfortably off did not last and Churchill's chronic appetite for the good things of life made inroads into his capital.

Nor, alas, was that the only injury suffered at this time. In December 1931 Churchill was in New York, preparing for another extensive speaking tour to no less than 40 US cities, a tour which might go some way to restoring his shattered finances, when he was struck by a taxicab while crossing Fifth Avenue. Churchill sustained two cracked ribs and numerous cuts and abrasions, which kept him laid up until the end of January 1932. Then he resumed the tour, visiting about half the cities on the original itinerary and returned to England in March, to find more journalism awaiting him and a major new commission – a *History of the English Speaking Peoples*, which he began in December 1932 and did not complete until 1957. The reason for this delay can be attributed to one man – the Nazi demagogue, Adolph Hitler, who became Chancellor of Germany in 1933.

The German people backed Hitler's rise to power; his success was no coup. In the elections for the German Parliament, the *Reichstag*, in 1928, the Nazis won only 12 seats. In 1932 they captured 230 seats and

Hindenburg was obliged to offer Hitler the post of Reich Chancellor, which he took up in January 1933. The first concentration camp at Dachau, a suburb of Munich, opened three months later.

Churchill had always been a foe of totalitarian regimes, whether of the Right or Left. He was against the Bolshevik activities in Russia but his opposition to the Nazis was equally vehement and was re-inforced by his early realisation of where Hitler was heading – towards a Europe dominated by Aryan racist ideology, backed by massive military force. It is fair to add that there was a brief window in the 1920s when Churchill saw some merit in the policies of Mussolini, largely because his actions at the time in tackling Italy's chronic problems was a great contrast to the drift that infected the British political scene at this time – but Churchill was a democrat and soon became fully aware of what the Fascist dictators were planning.

Churchill's answer to this growing totalitarian threat was firm opposition backed with rearmament, a position he maintained in the teeth of resistance from the 'appeasers,' three successive Prime Ministers: Ramsay MacDonald, Stanley Baldwin, and Neville Chamberlain, half-brother of Austen Chamberlain.

This is not to say that any of these gentlemen approved of Hitler's actions – far from it. Their conciliatory attitude towards Hitler had three main causes. First, that almost anything was better than a re-run of the First World War. Second, a somewhat naive belief that the realities of office would soon curb Nazi extremism. Finally, the fact that the economic situation simply did not permit the kind of massive re-armament that Churchill advocated.

The public tended to support appeasement. There was simply no appetite for another bloodbath, a point made by a vote in the Oxford Union, a student body, in February 1933 when the majority supported the motion that, *This House declines to fight for King and Country.* It should be mentioned that when war came six years later, these students and their successors at the time, flocked into the Services and died in great numbers for their country. Public support for appeasement lasted longer in Downing Street and Whitehall than it did in the country at large.

There was also more than a touch of isolationism in the British view of Continental affairs – that these problems in Central and Eastern Europe had nothing to do with Britain. This view was encapsulated in 1938 by the Prime Minister, Neville Chamberlain, with his comment that *'How horrible, fantastic, incredible it is that we should be digging trenches and trying on gas masks here because of a quarrel in a far away country between people of whom we know nothing.'*

Churchill had no sympathy with this view. Warfare had changed since 1914, and if the European democracies fought a war to avoid domination by the Fascists there was no way that Britain – or the US – could eventually avoid becoming involved. If Fascism triumphed in Austria and Czechoslovakia and stamped out the nascent democracy in Germany, it would eventually extinguish the light of freedom wherever it burned.

All that apart, the root of Naziism was naked Aryan racism, notably towards the Jews but embracing all other races the Nazis viewed as lesser breeds – *untermenchen*. Churchill was in no doubt, from the first moment he saw it, that Naziism was a doctrine that had to be resisted – a point confirmed by the German enactment of the Nuremberg Laws, which denied Jews any civil rights and made them not citizens but simply subjects of the State.

This view was not always popular. In May 1935 Churchill was rebuked in the House of Commons for making a speech that was, said one critic, *'Permeated with the atmosphere that Germany is preparing for war.'* The fact that Germany was preparing for war, in defiance of the Versailles Treaty, appears to have escaped this critic's notice. Criticism did not daunt Churchill or prevent him continuing to point out, in Parliament and in his journalism, that Germany was a growing threat to the peace of Europe.

Churchill was not alone in this; other leading British politicians – Harold McMillan, Duff Cooper, Bob Boothby, and Anthony Eden among them – were also constantly drawing attention to Hitler's intentions. Their view gained credibility when Hitler's troops re-occupied the Rhineland, demilitarised at Versailles, in 1936. Nor were the British at large overly impressed by the actions of von Ribbentrop, the German Ambassador to London between 1936-39 who, when calling at Buckingham Palace to present his papers, greeted King George VI with the Nazi salute.

A further erosion of the belief in Hitler's good intentions took place in 1936 with German support for Franco in the Spanish Civil War and the bombing of Guernica by the German-manned and equipped Condor Legion. Churchill had been agitating in particular about the obsolescent aircraft serving in the RAF and it was in 1936 that specifications were drawn up for the Spitfire and Hurricane fighters that would fight and win the Battle of Britain four years later – as well as for better bombers for RAF Bomber Command.

In the same year there was also one major distraction: the Abdication crisis. Following the death of King George V, his son the Prince of Wales should have ascended the Throne as Edward VIII. Prince Edward, however, had contracted a liaison with a twice-divorced American lady, Wallis Simpson, and declined to give her up. It was deemed impossible for the King of England and the Head of the Anglican Church to marry a divorced woman, and Edward VIII duly abdicated and was replaced with his younger brother, the Duke of York, who came to the Throne as George VI. This turned out to be no bad thing, since George VI was a far better man than his brother and would serve his people well in the years ahead.

Fascism was on the march in the middle years of the 1930s. Mussolini's Italy invaded Abyssinia in 1935, General Francisco Franco rebelled against the Republican Government of Spain in 1937, but the crucial year was 1938. In 1938 Hitler invaded Austria, and the union – the *Anschluss* – of these two countries, denied in 1919, was finally achieved. The Nazis' entry into Vienna was accompanied by another attack on the Jews who were already being driven out of Germany in large numbers, forfeiting all their possessions before being allowed to leave.

The democratic powers, a shrinking number, did nothing about the invasion of Abyssinia, and adopted a policy of 'non-intervention' in Spain – a policy observed only by Britain and France. Italy and Germany sent aid to Franco and Soviet Russia sent arms to the Republic, in return for Communist domination of Republican affairs. Everywhere, the democrats were on the retreat.

It was apparent to all, certainly to Churchill and anyone who heard him speak or read his newspaper articles, that appeasing dictators simply increased their appetite for concessions. Emboldened by his uncontested actions in the Rhineland and Austria, Hitler now turned on Czechoslovakia where the Germans of the Sudetenland – a minority left on the Czechoslovak border by the self-determination policies of Versailles – were deemed to be persecuted by the Czechs and in need of German protection.

Churchill deemed this crisis so gravely that he cancelled a speaking tour in the US, though his funds were so depleted that he was forced to put Chartwell on the market. But for the fortunate intervention of a South African millionaire who bought Churchill's declining investment portfolio at its original value, the Churchills might have found themselves without a home, but this domestic problem did not distract him from wider issues. Chamberlain flew twice to Germany and met Hitler face to face at Berchtesgaden but to no avail; the French and British were not prepared to go to war to save the Czechs and in the absence of such a step Hitler first took over the Sudetenland and then the entire country – nothing was done to prevent this crime in either London or Paris.

Indeed, Chamberlain even attempted to present the Munich Agreement – the betrayal of Czechoslovakia – as a diplomatic triumph. This attempt failed. Duff Cooper and Anthony Eden resigned from the Government over Munich and Churchill was scathing when he rose to speak in the subsequent debate, rejecting any notion that the Munich Agreement was any kind of triumph; quite the contrary.

'We have sustained a total and unmitigated defeat,' said Churchill,

'and France has suffered even more than we have... all that the exertions of the Prime Minister have been able to secure is that the German dictator, instead of snatching the victuals from the table, has been content to have them served up to him, course by course.'

Some defensive steps were now taken. Following Hitler's invasion of Czechoslovakia and the *Kristalnacht* attack on the German Jews in November 1938, and especially after the rump of Czechoslovakia was occupied by the Wehrmacht in March 1939, the scales fell from Chamberlain's eyes. Belatedly, Britain began to rearm. Conscription was introduced, the Territorial Army expanded, and volunteers flocked into the Auxiliary squadrons of the RAF. The question now was where Hitler would strike next and the balance of informed opinion suggested that the Nazis' next victim would be Poland.

Poland offered German aggression all the usual ingredients: a substantial German minority, the loss of East Prussia at Versailles, and the existence of the 'Polish Corridor' through German territory and up to the port of Danzig. All were 'anomalies' that Hitler resolved to end. In addition the Poles were regarded as *untermenschen* and their territory suitable for that *lebensraum* – the living space – that Germany's growing population demanded.

Aware of Hitler's intention, the British and French Governments issued guarantees to Poland, assuring the Poles that they would come to her aid if attacked. There were two snags with these promises. First, exactly how were the British and French supposed to aid a country like Poland, so far from their own frontiers except over sea lanes dominated by Germany? Second, after the climb downs over the Rhineland, Austria and Czechoslovakia, Hitler was not remotely convinced that this time the two Western Allies would stand firm against him.

Throughout the summer Churchill continued to speak out against Hitler, and he now had a ready audience, including newspaper editorials demanding that Churchill be included in the Government, yet there was no response from Chamberlain.

There was one final hope for the Poles – not a happy one but an obvious one, not least because of the chronic hostility between the Nazis and the Communists – that in the event of attack, Soviet Russia would come to her aid or ally herself with the Western Powers. This hope was fleeting; the Nazis and the Communists saw the destruction of the democracies and the partition of Poland as in their immediate interest and in August 1939, in Moscow, the Foreign Ministers of Russia and Germany, Molotov and Ribbentrop signed a Nazi-Soviet Non-Aggression Pact which, among other clauses, provided for the division of Poland between these rival totalitarian powers.

Two weeks later, on 1 September, 1939, Germany and Russia invaded Poland – but Hitler had miscalculated. This time Britain and France were serious. On 2 September they demanded that Germany withdraw her troops from Poland and at 11:00am on 3 September, 1939, no answer having been received from Berlin, Neville Chamberlain came on the radio to tell the British people that they were at war with Germany.

8. Return to Power

1939 - 1940

'*Winston is Back*'

Signal from the Admiralty to the Ships of the Royal Navy,
September 3, 1939

Britain's declaration of war with Germany, made at 11am on 3
September, 1939, provided a bitter moment for Prime Minister Neville
Chamberlain. He had tried for years to avoid this situation and
sacrificed a great deal of political capital and his personal reputation for
firm and fair dealing in the process – apart from abandoning the people
of Czechoslovakia. His policies now lay in ruins and he was confronted
by an aggressive, well-equipped power. Britain was currently in no
condition to fight, and the blame for that unprepared situation could
also be laid at Chamberlain's door.

As the appeasement policy of the 1930's ended in failure and left
Britain in a parlous state in 1939, Chamberlain has since come to be
regarded as a pathetic, irresolute figure, whose actions actually contributed to the outbreak of the Second World War. There is some truth

127

in this, but not much. Neville Chamberlain was by no means alone in his willingness to temporise with the Fascists.

Outside the Fascist powers – Germany, Italy, perhaps Spain – there was no eagerness for war in Europe, no sense among the democratic powers that the only way to repel aggression was by an equal display of power, or at the very least a willingness to fight. Indeed, when Chamberlain returned from Munich in 1938 and declared that his agreement with Hitler offered *'peace in our time'* his comment was widely applauded. Pacifism was in vogue in Britain, much of Europe and the US; re-armament was seen as provocative. In most political quarters, Chamberlain's appeasement stance was popular and Churchill's warnings ignored.

As the war clouds gathered after Munich, Chamberlain's Government had begun to re-arm and the nation braced itself for the war that most people knew was coming, with many joining the Auxilary Air Force or the Territorial Army. Unable to grasp that fact, Chamberlain still tried to avoid bringing Churchill back into Government, and was certainly against offering him a place in the War Cabinet. Now, with the outbreak of war, such a step was inevitable. Churchill had been saying for years that this moment would come, that another European war was inevitable unless German aggression was resisted.

Now it had come and the public and the Press were clamouring loudly for Churchill's return to the Government benches. Hitler's vindication of Churchill's views by the attack on Poland on 1 September, 1939, demanded Churchill's return to office, and clearly to an office where he could have a direct influence on the course of wartime events. Therefore, on the afternoon of 1 September, Chamberlain bowed to the inevitable and offered Churchill both a seat in the War Cabinet and his old First World War post as First Lord of the Admiralty.

Churchill accepted both positions with alacrity. He sent a telegram to the Admiralty in Whitehall saying he would arrive later that day and begin his task with a staff meeting and in particular with the professional head of the Royal Navy, the First Sea Lord, Admiral Sir Dudley

Pound – hence that signal sent by the Admiralty to the Fleet where the news of Churchill's appointment was received with considerable jubilation.

However, as in the previous war – indeed, in all his political appointments – Churchill had no intention of restricting his activities to his own duties, however extensive and onerous, or confining his interests to his own department. The War Cabinet met daily, sometimes twice a day, and Churchill was one of the most vocal members, always advocating action. At the first meeting of the War Cabinet on September 4, he proposed an Anglo-French attack on the Siegfried Line, the Western bastion of Germany, an attack which, said Churchill, should be supported with the full strength of the RAF. This proposal was rejected but Churchill was not deterred. A stream of notes offering advice or suggestions flowed from his office to his colleagues, especially the Foreign Secretary, Lord Halifax, and the Prime Minister, Neville Chamberlain.

The first weeks of the war in 1939 saw the destruction of Poland by a new kind of campaign, a sweeping advance based on the rapid forward movement of German tanks and infantry, supported by artillery and dive bombers and therefore known as *blitzkrieg,* or lightning war. Fifty-six German divisions, many of them armoured, poured into Poland where the Poles were often obliged to attack the German tanks on horseback, armed with swords and lances, with predictable results.

The Polish Air Force was destroyed in two days and by the end of the second week the Polish Army – some 2 million men – had effectively ceased to exist as a fighting force. Then the Soviets took a hand in this squalid invasion, anxious to collect the spoils promised by the Ribbentrop-Molotov Pact. The Russian Red Army attacked from the east and met their German counterparts at Brest-Litovsk – the place where the German-Russian Peace Treaty, so damaging to Russia, had been arranged in 1917. Warsaw fell on 19 September after an attack by German bombers and on 29 September the Germans and Russians signed a Treaty partitioning Poland. By that time, barely three weeks into this six-year war the German SS *Einsatzgruppen* – murder squads – were already at work in western Poland, rounding up and murdering Polish Jews, seizing Polish property, killing anyone who resisted.

The fall of Poland and in particular the actions of Soviet Russia made a deep impression on Winston Churchill, one that he never forgot. The French and British guarantees to Poland, which could not be implemented in 1939, remained in Churchill's mind throughout the war and were to appear again when he confronted the Soviets, by then one of the Allies, at Yalta in 1945.

Churchill told the British public in a BBC broadcast on 1 October, 1939:

> '*I cannot forecast to you the actions of Russia. It is a riddle wrapped in a mystery inside an enigma: but perhaps there is a key. That key is Russian national interest. It cannot be in accordance with the interest of the safety of Russia that Germany should plant itself on the shores of the Black Sea or overrun the Balkans or subjugate the Slavonic peoples of South Eastern Europe.*'

Churchill was thinking ahead. He did not believe that this alliance of totalitarian powers could last, and he was right. Since neither dictator had any moral core, it was inevitable that, sooner or later, they would fall out or one would betray the other.

Churchill's broadcast, and his other, self-appointed role as a Government spokesman was quite apart from the work piling up at the Admiralty. Most of this concerned the U-boat submarine menace, which had manifested itself on the first day of the war with the sinking of the passenger liner *Athenia,* off the north west coast of Ireland by the *U-30*. The *Athenia* was taking evacuees, mostly women and children, from Britain to the US and 112 were lost, including 28 Americans. So began a campaign that was to last for the rest of the war and cost an immense number of ships and lives. The loss of the *Athenia* also brought home to the Government that unless the seaways could be kept open, Britain was doomed to die of starvation.

Fortunately the German Navy only had 58 U-boats in commission at the start of the war, of which only 39 were at sea, and these were forced to operate from bases on the North Sea coast and the Baltic. Admiral Doenitz, the commander of the German U-Boat fleet, had wanted 300 submarines in commission before the outbreak of war but Hitler had insisted on diverting the shipyards to the construction of capital ships and surface vessels. Had these 300 U-boats been available in 1939, Britain could not have survived. *'The only thing that really frightened me during the War'*, said Churchill later, *'was the submarine menace.'*

The lessons of the First World War had not been forgotten. The first step to countering the submarines was the introduction of the convoy system and the provision of convoy escorts. The British Merchant Navy had 2,000 ships at sea at any one time and the convoy system was both the best way to protect them and of finding and sinking U-boats. These were hard to find in the open ocean but tended to gather in the sea-lanes where some were detected. This concentration on convoy protection resulted in the sinking of two U-boats before the end of September but 53 British ships were lost in that month, 41 of them sunk by U-Boats.

The first convoys sailed from British ports on 7 September but the problem at this stage was a shortage of small, fast, convoy escorts. Due to a shortage of warships, especially sloops, frigates, and destroyers, the Royal Navy could only protect shipping to and from 12.5 degrees West; beyond that line the merchant ships were on their own and the convoys broke up, the faster ships steaming hard for the safety of US waters, the slower ships hoping to avoid U-boats in the wide Atlantic. This problem was eased somewhat on 5 September, when the US declared its neutral status in this war but began naval patrols to protect shipping inside US territorial waters.

Nor were submarines the only menace Churchill and his captains had to deal with. At the start of October the German pocket battleship *Graf Spee* broke into the Atlantic and went in search of British shipping. Not many were found; before *Graf Spee* was found and engaged by a

British cruiser squadron she had sunk only 9 small ships, a total loss of some 50,000 tons. On 14 October, a German submarine, U-47, made a daring incursion into the British naval base at Scapa Flo and sank the old battleship *Royal Oak*. This was not a serious loss but it indicated a flaw in harbour protection and was a considerable embarrassment to the new First Lord.

Churchill was already extremely busy and slipping into the daily routine that was to occupy his time throughout the war, and prove a sore trial to his personal advisers and close associates. Churchill was now 65, retirement age for most people, but by taking a short nap of one or two hours in the middle of the afternoon he was able to keep working until one or two in the morning, fitting two days work into one. This went on, night after night, for weeks on end, wearing out a succession of secretaries who came to work in shifts to cope with his demands, and exhausting his military and naval advisers who had worked throughout the day and now found that they had to be on hand during the night.

Apart from keeping his Cabinet colleagues on their toes and bombarding the Fleet with urgent memoranda – many bearing the sticker marked '*Action This Day*,' Churchill also began corresponding with the US President, Franklin D. Roosevelt. For this correspondence – which should properly have come from the Prime Minister, Neville Chamberlain – Churchill used the code name '*Naval Person*.' When he became Prime Minister Churchill changed this to '*Former Naval Person*,' one that he was to employ in his correspondence with Roosevelt for the rest of the war.

The President, not Churchill, initiated this correspondence. It took place over the head of Mr Chamberlain who knew about it, but was content to let it continue, trusting Churchill to let him know about any interesting exchanges. Relations between Churchill and Chamberlain were good at this time, not least because Churchill was handling the Prime Minister with considerable tact, even checking the content of his speeches with the Prime Minister's office before presenting them in the House or on the BBC.

These speeches carried an upbeat message to Parliament and public. On 29 September Churchill regaled the House with the actions of the Royal Navy in the last three weeks, claiming that six or seven U-boats had already been sunk (the actual total was two) and delighting his audience with anecdotes:

> '*From time to time the German U-boat commanders have tried their best to behave with humanity... One German captain signalled to me personally the position of a British vessel he had just sunk and urged me that rescue should be sent. I was in some doubt at the time to what address I should direct a reply. However, he is now in our hands and being treated with all consideration.*'

These speeches were for public consumption; privately Churchill knew there was little cause for satisfaction with Britain's military state or the progress of the war – and the war at sea was hotting-up. On 21 November, the brand new and heavily armed cruiser, *HMS Belfast,* was damaged by a magnetic mine in the Firth of Forth in Scotland. The magnetic mine was another menace to British shipping and it was some months before a counter-measure could be developed.

Two days later, on 23 November, the German battlecruiser *Scharnhorst* found a British convoy guarded by just one escort, the armed merchant ship *Rawalpindi*. Though hopelessly outgunned, *Rawalpindi* turned to engage the enemy while the convoy scattered and was duly sunk with heavy loss of life among the crew. On 4 December, another British warship, the battleship *HMS Nelson,* was damaged by a magnetic mine.

So German submarines and surface raiders continued to chip away at the might of the British Fleet, including the far-flung Merchant Fleet. By the end of December 1939, 79 British merchantmen had been lost – a total of 262,000 tons, with considerable loss of life among the crews. On the other hand, the British blockade of Germany was also taking its toll; 325 German ships, totalling some 750,00 tons of shipping, were penned up in German ports, unable to go to sea because of Royal Navy patrols.

Before Christmas Churchill was able to come to the House with some good news. On 19 December, Commodore Harwood, flying his flag in the cruiser *HMS Exeter* with the light cruisers *Ajax* and *Achilles* in company, had found and engaged the German battle cruiser *Graf Spee* in the South Atlantic. *Graf Spee's* radar-controlled 11-inch guns far outranged the 8- and 6-inch guns on the British cruisers, and in a two-hour engagement all three British ships were badly damaged. They did not, however, break off the action; the Nelson spirit still dominated the Royal Navy and *Graf Spee* had also sustained hits.

Harried by two of the British warships – one had gone off, badly damaged, to the Falkland Islands – the German commander, Captain Langsdorff, took his ship into the neutral port of Montevideo to effect repairs. While he was there, *Ajax* and *Achilles* took station off the mouth of the Plate, ready to resume the action, being joined later by the heavy cruiser *HMS Cumberland*. For some still-unknown reason, Langsdorff declined to come out and fight, scuttled *Graf Spee* in the Montevideo roads, and shot himself.

The destruction of the *Graf Spee* boosted the nation's morale and did a great deal for Churchill's standing. His office, the Admiralty, were seen to be actively prosecuting the war at a time when the Army was stuck in France, where nothing was happening and RAF operations against Germany were hampered by Government restrictions – that no shore targets could be bombed for example – and the inadequacy of their aircraft.

While these actions were taking place on the oceans, Churchill had also been busy nearer home. On 9 September, one week into the war, the first troops of the British Expeditionary Force, just four divisions, were conveyed across the Channel without loss. Churchill had been responsible for the passage of the first BEF to France in 1914 and was proud to have done this again in 1939, and again without loss. The War Cabinet were also discussing ways in which this slender force could be expanded to a total of 55 divisions but every arm of the Services was crying out for men, equipment, and supplies which Britain's war factories were hard pressed to supply.

Meanwhile the Empire was mustering to the defence of the Mother Country. The first message of support and aid came early on 3 September, 1939, from the tiny Caribbean island of Barbados. Every day thereafter more messages came flooding in as the men and women of Australia, New Zealand, Canada, and South Africa flocked to the Colours. They were quickly followed by India – over two million Indian soldiers joined the Armies of the *Raj* in the Second World War and every one was a volunteer – there was no conscription in India. To the British muster came soldiers from East and West Africa, from the islands of the Caribbean and the British communities in South America, most notably from Chile. Gurkhas came from Nepal – over 80,000 of them – plus a great number of men from the Irish Free State – and not a few Americans, many crossing the border into Canada to join the Royal Canadian Air Force.

As in the First World War Churchill was an aggressive war leader, not content merely to parry the German blows but anxious to retaliate. Keeping within his own naval remit, Churchill proposed sending a landing force, accompanied by two battleships, to raid the German Baltic coast, a notion his advisors hastened to discourage since air power was now a factor in strategy and the *Luftwaffe* would have swiftly sent these ships to the bottom of the sea. Allowing his mind full range, Churchill remembered another task undertaken at the end of the First World War and was able to tell Chamberlain that he had located a large quantity of artillery, which, as Minister of Munitions, he had stored away in 1919. If obsolescent, these guns were still in good repair and could be used for coastal defence. Almost 400 heavy artillery pieces – 12-inch, 9-inch, 8-inch and 6-inch guns – were quickly added to Britain's defences.

Churchill's other activities included moves to improve the defences of the naval base at Scapa Flo and attempts to speed up the construction of naval escorts; 32 Fleet destroyers were currently under construction but only nine would be delivered before the end of 1940 which was much too far away. Something smaller and capable of more rapid construction was needed and this was found by expanding the corvette programme – small, heavily armed anti-submarine craft capable of crossing the Atlantic. Orders for 50 of these handy little ships, the first of the famous *Flower* class corvettes, had been placed in early 1939 but as yet only a few had emerged from the yards.

Here again one of Churchill's urgent memoranda was called for. This urgent search for destroyer escorts would eventually lead to a call on America, Churchill asking for 50 old US destroyers, currently in mothballs, to bridge the gap until the British destroyers and corvettes could enter service. The first request was refused, as the United States was still in the grip of isolationism and had no wish to provoke the Germans at this time.

Churchill also considered proposals for cutting the supply line from Norway that brought high-grade iron ore from Sweden to Germany. Above all he sought to speed the equipping of Bomber Command with aircraft and those navigation and target-finding aids capable of carrying the war to Germany and smiting the industrial cities of the Ruhr.

Churchill reported on all these activities to the House in encouraging speeches that raised morale and spirits. Churchill stated his firm conviction that while the struggle would be long and hard all that was necessary to win this war was a great deal of perseverance. After the hesitations of Neville Chamberlain, this was heartening news and Churchill's reputation soared, not least within the ranks of the Tory Party. Churchill was to repeat this message to the public in his first radio broadcast, recounting the progress of the Royal Navy to date but adding that, '*the war might last for at least three years but Britain would fight to the end and win, convinced we are the defenders of civilisation and freedom.*'

This public declaration of a willingness to continue the fight was underlined on October 6 when Hitler, speaking in Berlin, offered to negotiate with the French and British - provided they first agreed to Germany's occupation of Czechoslovakia and Poland. Speaking in Cabinet, Churchill urged his colleagues to reject these proposals and any other proposals until '*the sovereignty and territorial integrity of these nations had been fully restored.'* The mood of the country at this time was fully in support of Churchill's views but there were those in Parliament who were less sanguine; fully aware of Britain's military weakness, these people did not see *how* the country could prosecute this war and were willing, though not eager, to listen to German proposals.

Churchill was fully determined to block any movement towards a negotiated peace, partly because he did not believe anything Hitler said, partly because it would legitimate Nazi aggression, mainly because he was fundamentally opposed to totalitarianism in any form and had no intention of permitting any back-sliding towards 1930's appeasement now the shooting war had started.

The appeasers had been silent but they had not gone away. Although there was little likelihood that their quiet, siren calls for 'peace at any price' would attract any measure of public support, there was always the possibility that the usual political belief – that politicians always know better than the public – might turn Britain back onto the path that leads towards conciliation. Churchill's voice, confident, lively, aggressive, was a useful public counterweight to any behind-the-scenes muttering from people like Rab Butler and the Foreign Secretary, Lord Halifax, both of whom expressed high-toned distaste for Churchill's strong and patriotic speeches.

There were other issues. Britain's difficulties in the Atlantic convoy battles would have been eased had the Royal Navy been able to use the four Treaty Ports in Ireland retained for their use in the 1921 Anglo-Irish Treaty, but that right had been surrendered in 1938. The Irish Government now refused the Royal Navy access, and allowed the Nazi Government to operate a large embassy in Dublin.

Another problem was that flow of high-grade iron ore from Sweden to Germany, much of it shipped from the neutral Norwegian port of Narvik. Churchill's desire to end this traffic in strategic materials led directly to his next major venture, the Norwegian campaign of 1940. Among Churchill's reasons for embarking on this campaign was a desire to get on with the war – and, or so it was said, to remove the old stigma of the failed attempt at the Dardanelles in 1915.

Other than at sea and, within certain weather and operational restraints in the air, the war had come to a halt. This was the period that later became known as the *Phoney War,* when the German and Anglo-French armies stared at each other across the Western Front but refrained from all but patrol activity. This was a situation the French were happy to continue, favouring operations elsewhere, anything not to provoke the Germans into an all-out *blitzkrieg* against France.

This Phoney War did offer the Allies certain advantages – their men were training, their factories gearing up to war production – but Churchill for one was under no illusion about Hitler's intentions. The *Führer* was using these winter months to either unnerve his opponents or weaken their resolve with offers of conciliation, and switch his forces west from Poland. Since any large-scale military operations would be difficult in the winter, as low cloud cover inhibited the use of dive bombers in *blitzkrieg* operations, this biding time was useful and cost Hitler nothing. If the Allies were still intransigent and refused to settle for his offers come the Spring, he could smite them hard.

Churchill was often in France, urging Britain's allies into action in his unique blend of French and English – *'Nous allons perdre l'omnibus'* ('We are going to miss the bus') – being one colloquial English phrase that certainly baffled his hosts. Churchill considered it necessary to regain the initiative and strike first but could get no support in Parliament or from the French. Therefore, in lieu of action in France, the Royal Navy struck at Norway on 8 April, 1940, in the first combined operation of the war.

Unfortunately, the Germans struck first. German forces, spear-headed by the *Luftwaffe,* invaded Denmark and crossed the narrow sea to Norway. The force, speed, and co-ordination of the German advance outmatched anything the British could manage, and with the *Luftwaffe* on the spot and quickly controlling the skies the outcome of the Norwegian campaign was not long in doubt. The Norwegian action cost the German Navy a number of warships; three German cruisers and ten destroyers were sunk and others damaged. But Britain's naval losses were not insignificant; eleven ships were sunk, including the aircraft carrier *HMS Glorious*, and many others damaged.

Taken as a whole, the Norwegian campaign was a British defeat. The landing force had to be evacuated under heavy air attack barely two weeks after going ashore and nothing significant had been achieved, except a display of resolution and a willingness to fight. Strangely, although he had been the instigator of this campaign, very little odium was attached to Churchill for this failure – this was not a re-run of the Gallipoli debacle. The public and the House of Commons knew that Churchill was willing to fight this war and as long as he was fighting, any setbacks could be forgiven.

On the other hand, should Chamberlain topple, it was by no means certain at this time that Churchill would be his automatic successor. Norway did not damage Churchill's reputation but it did not help him much either. Other men – notably Lord Halifax, the Foreign Secretary – were regarded in the House of Commons as sounder politicians. On the other hand, Halifax was a member of the House of Lords. Although ways could be found to get round this obstacle and enable the noble lord to speak in the Commons, it was a snag that Churchill's supporters never ceased to point out.

The Norwegian campaign was the subject of a two-day debate in the House on the 7th-8th May, 1940. This debate was the occasion for the expression of general discontent with the actions of the Government and the conduct of the war, though the complaints made by Clement Attlee, the Leader of the Opposition, that: '*Norway comes as the culmination of many other discontents…everywhere the story is "Too Late,"'* significantly failed to make any criticism of Churchill. The same was true of the other major speeches by other leading figures but it fell to Leo Amery, a backbench MP, to deliver the most telling blow against Neville Chamberlain's administration and being it down.

After listing all the past failures of resolve, Amery recalled Oliver Cromwell's words when dismissing the Long Parliament during the English Civil War, concluding his attack by using Cromwell's own damming injunction: '*You have sat too long for any good you have been*

doing. Depart, I say, and let us have done with you. In God's name, Go!'
The effect of this speech on the House was electrifying – and Chamberlain was doomed.

On the second day of this debate the attacks on Chamberlain's record continued, turning the debate into a Vote of Censure, and came to a head when the Prime Minister accepted the challenge to his policies and called on the House to put the matter to the vote, telling the House that 'he expected his friends to join him in the lobbies' (where the Yes and No votes are counted). This declaration proved another serious mistake.

Although there were many abstentions on the Conservative side – Party loyalty remained strong and only 486 out of the 615 MPs present voted at all – 41 Tories voted against the Government. The outcome was a narrow rejection of the vote of censure by just 81 votes. In normal times, this would have been a more than adequate majority and been hailed as an endorsement of Government policy but these were not normal times – and the 41 MPs who had voted against their party were only the tip of a wider discontent, as many more abstained from voting at all. That night Chamberlain called Churchill to Downing Street and told him that he did not think he could go on.

Had this reverse in the North and in the House been all it would have been bad enough for the British Government, but the *Wehrmacht* was on the march again. On 10 May, 1940, two days after this debate, the German Army swept west and over-ran Holland and Belgium. On that day Chamberlain called Halifax and Churchill to a meeting, the purpose of which, he told them, was to discuss who should succeed him as Prime Minister.

Chamberlain's choice was clearly for Lord Halifax and he tried to nudge Churchill into voicing support for this notion, hoping that Churchill would agree to Halifax taking over. Churchill for once remained silent, gazing out the window into the park, letting the silence drag on. At last it was Halifax who broke. Declaring that as a peer, he would be unable to take part in Commons debates, he declined to stand and so the succession passed to Churchill. Now was his hour, the moment Churchill had been waiting for, the job he had always wanted at last in his grasp. It could not have come at a more difficult time, and it remained to be seen what he would do with it.

9. A Time of Trial

May 1940 - December 1941

'Now at last the slowly-gathered, long pent-up fury of the storm broke upon us.'

Winston S. Churchill

Churchill came to power at a most difficult time. By June 1940 the country was *in extremis,* with disaster looming on every side and few successes to bolster morale. The Norwegian campaign had been little short of a fiasco. German submarines were sinking British shipping in the North Atlantic. The RAF bomber offensive against Germany was an obvious failure. Daylight operations had proved costly with losses of up to fifty percent among the aircrews; night raids were inaccurate and doing no damage to German industry. The Army was still severely under strength and short of modern weapons; much of it was deployed in France awaiting Germany's next move, which came with devastating force on May 10, 1940, when the Phoney War ended abruptly.

As First Lord of the Admiralty, Churchill could have been held responsible for at least some of these continuing reverses but although the Norway debacle brought down Neville Chamberlain, the critics of Chamberlain's policies were careful to exclude Churchill from this general condemnation. Churchill had enemies but his willingness to fight had never been doubted. The British have a saying: 'Cometh the Hour, Cometh the Man.' This was Churchill's hour and everyone knew it.

Certainly Churchill knew it. Writing of this time later, he said, '*All my past life had been but a preparation for this hour and this trial and I was sure I would not fail.*'

A review of Churchill's previous life, as already detailed in these pages, reveals that there is truth in that conviction. If the ability to take charge of events at a difficult time requires a certain blend of experience and character, Churchill's life so far had provided that experience and formed his character, but some of the essential qualities – courage, tenacity, a sense of humour – he had been born with.

He had known tragedy and personal loss – not least in the untimely death of his father and one of his children. He was not wealthy and had to work hard for all he possessed, and lost a lot of it through bad luck or poor advice. He had made many mistakes – at Gallipoli, in Parliament, in his choice of friends and policies, but he had rarely made the same mistake twice. He had matured steadily but retained certain basic qualities, of which courage was the most obvious and at the present time the most useful.

He had the ability to empathise with all classes and reserved a strong and enduring affection for the ordinary Briton, the man in the street – or trench, gun turret, or cockpit. He was capable of holding his own in the Cabinet and the House of Commons, and he also had the knack of addressing the public at large in words that filled their hearts and made their spirits soar, expressing beliefs that they could understand and be willing to die for.

Churchill had many faults but he had great virtues: courage, a clear sense of right and wrong, a determination not to compromise with tyranny, a belief that right would triumph in the end. Above all, he had a willingness to lead, to take the initiative in this fast-spreading war and fight it out to the end. This was no political ploy or assumed attitude; the times were too serious for any of that. If Churchill failed in his task

Britain was lost. Churchill had another great asset, the product of his background – great self-confidence and a boundless belief in his own abilities.

These too had been in evidence in his early life. Churchill did not waste his time with underlings or in beating about the bush with intermediaries. He went straight to the top to ask for what he wanted and never felt the slightest qualm in pressing his advice and opinions on his colleagues and superiors or showing the slightest resentment when his views were rejected. In this dark hour, his approach was set forth as follows:

'In war; Resolution
In defeat; Defiance
In victory; Magnanimity
In peace; Goodwill.'

Throughout the Second World War he never deviated from this formula. The period from May 1940 to December 1941 made Winston Churchill one of the great men of the twentieth century – perhaps *the* great man – and certainly one of the 'Great Men' of history.

But for that time of trial he might be remembered, if at all, as someone who never quite matched up to his full potential, one of those tragic figures 'it is just too bad about,' a man who never had the chance to show what he was made of, or made a mess of his numerous opportunities. As it was, his resolute actions and, above all, his speeches in the dark days of Dunkirk and the Blitz, provided the basis for the future legend and consolidated Churchill's position as a truly great figure.

Two decades later, John F.Kennedy, the President of the United States said that Churchill in 1940 *'mustered the English language and sent it into battle.'* This was useful for at the time Britain had very little else to fight with.

Thanks to the policy of appeasement, gross under-investment in the military and the dire effects of the Ten Year Rule until well into the

1930's, when the war broke out Britain's armed forces were woefully inadequate in numbers and very short of good kit. RAF Fighter Command had the excellent Spitfire fighter and the adequate Hurricane but Bomber Command was short of aircraft and trained crews and lacked the navigation and target marking equipment needed to carry out its strategic task: the destruction of the military and industrial power of Germany. As for the Royal Navy, it had excellent capital ships – battleships and cruisers – but was short of convoy escorts and aircraft carriers and very short of submarine detection equipment (Asdic, or Anti-Submarine Detection) and any way to tackle the menace of mines.

The biggest deficits were in the Army and especially, and most critically, in the armoured and anti-tank forces, which must face and beat the powerful German *panzer* forces. The tank units had the slow, under-gunned Matilda infantry tank, top speed 8 miles per hour, equipped with a short-range 2-pounder gun; the anti-tank units had the Boyes anti-tank rifle and some 2-pounder anti-tank guns whose shells bounced off the frontal armour of the German *panzers*. In May 1940 Britain only had one armoured division in the west – there was another, the 7th Armoured Division, in Egypt facing the Italians – but that one was training in England and had only 328 tanks. The Germans had 10 fully equipped armoured divisions in the west, all with much better tanks.

A brief overview of the British Armed Forces at this time could have reported the situation in just eight words: too little, too late – and none of it good enough. As in the First World War, so it was again; the fighting men had to wait for adequate equipment. Not until the middle of 1942, three years into this war – and half-way through it for Britain and her Empire – would the British military get the men and equipment they needed to carry the fight to the enemy. That was the price paid for the peaceful policies of the inter-war years, and the British Empire and Commonwealth fighting men were the ones to pay that price on the battlefield.

In May 1940 the immediate future looked bleak, but words can be weapons too. Churchill's speeches came from the heart and struck home with the public. He did not conceal the gravity of the situation but spoke directly to the British people. They were fully determined to fight on and only needed that leadership so long denied them in the dreary years of appeasement.

This Churchill hastened to provide. His speeches from this time have remained classics of oratory, but they also remain close to the hearts of the British people, a surviving relic of the time when they stood alone against a mighty tyranny. This process began with Churchill's first speech as Prime Minister in the House of Commons on 13 May, 1940 – a speech short, unequivocal, and directly to the point:

> 'I would say to the House, as I have said to those who have joined this Government, that I have nothing to offer but blood, toil, tears and sweat. We have before us an ordeal of the most grievous kind. You ask, what is our policy? I will say – it is to wage war, by sea, land and air, with all the might and strength that God can give us – to wage war against a monstrous tyranny, never surpassed in the dark, lamentable catalogue of human crime. That is our policy'.
>
> 'You ask, what is our aim? I can answer in one word – Victory. Victory at all costs, victory in spite of all terror, victory, however long or hard the road may be, for without victory there is no survival...But I take up my task with buoyancy and hope. I feel sure that our cause will not be suffered to fail among men. At this time I feel entitled to claim the aid of all and I say "Come, let us go forward together, with all our united strength."'

The words are direct and stirring but they lose a great deal without the sound of Churchill's voice, rolling out the sentences – the second sentence in the first paragraph is typically Churchill – once heard, it echoes around the head before the speech moves on to stir the heart with those words of grim resolve.

The speech concludes with an appeal for national unity, one that had already been met; the Labour Party had now joined the National Coalition Government that was to fight the war – with Clement Attlee, the Labour leader, as Churchill's Deputy and Lord Privy Seal, Earnest Bevin at the vital post of Minister of Labour and National Service, Herbert Morrison as Minister of Supply, Hugh Dalton as Minister of Economic Warfare. Neville Chamberlain, though ill, remained in the Cabinet and Lord Halifax was retained as Foreign Secretary, though later sent as ambassador to Washington. Churchill, in addition to being Prime Minister and First Lord of the Treasury, the latter being always part of the Prime Minister's remit, retained the posts of Minister of Defence and Leader of the House of Commons. With these arrangements made, the battle for survival began.

Churchill and the British people would soon need all their resolve. Within days of Churchill taking office the German Armies in the West were on the move, rolling forward inexorably over Holland, Belgium and France, crushing all resistance with air power and tanks, employing again the techniques of *blitzkrieg* war that had been honed to perfection during Germany's 1939 campaign in Poland.

The summer of 1940 was a time of terror for the civilian population of Western Europe. The newsreels and newspapers of the time are full of photographs showing towns and villages on fire, long lines of refugees fleeing before the invader, women pushing carts and prams along country roads, savaged as they went by dive-bombing and machine-gunning aircraft.

Nor were the Allied soldiers in much better shape. The Franco-British Armies were quite unprepared for the weight, force and mobility of the German onslaught and had no weapons or tactics capable of resisting the powerful combination of tanks, heavy guns and dive-bombing aircraft the enemy deployed against them – the scream of the sirens on the German *Ju. 87 Stukas* as they wheeled and plunged like vultures over the Anglo-French forces is an abiding memory of that fatal summer.

However, while these military deficiencies certainly contributed to the rapid collapse of the Armies, nothing did so much to precipitate the rapid collapse of the Western governments as the sudden sharp decline of political will. The first country to collapse was Holland; this small country had no means to resist the kind of force Germany swung against it. The German Army broke through at various points along the frontier and poured along the flat Dutch roads. After Rotterdam was bombed and set on fire the Dutch surrendered, though many of their soldiers, sailors and airmen – and the Dutch Royal Family – came to Britain to continue the fight.

Belgium was the next to go. Belgians had clung to their neutrality and declined to join an alliance with Britain and France but, as in the First World War this did not save her from aggression and invasion. Her frontiers were quickly breached by a German thrust through the wooded hills of the Ardennes, which outflanked the fixed French defences of the Maginot Line – leaving the left flank of the British Expeditionary Force fully exposed. With the Belgian Army in full retreat and the Government on the point of collapse – it collapsed on 15 May – it was now the turn of France.

Churchill rapidly became aware that the French Government of M. Reynard was also contemplating surrender, dismayed by the outflanking of the Maginot Line. The Germans were now swarming into Northern France and those French divisions not engaged with the enemy were in full retreat. Churchill made regular visits to France in this period and was dismayed when the response to his query, *'Ou est la masse de manoeuvre'* ('where is the strategic reserve?'), General Gamelin, the French Commander-in-Chief, shrugged his shoulders and replied, *'Aucune'* ('there isn't one').

Churchill records that Gamelin's reply was a considerable blow to his hopes of a continued resistance in France. His request for an immediate counter-attack in the north to stem or slow the German advance was greeted with French scepticism, and no signs of action. Churchill and the British Army staff were staggered that the French Commander-in-Chief and the leading French Government were already convinced that all was lost – and this within days of the German attack. This information was accompanied with a request – a demand – from France that the British should commit more troops and all their front-line RAF fighter squadrons to the battle in France.

To comply with the first part of the request was simply not possible; Britain had no more trained troops to send and little to equip them with. As for sending more fighters, given the present state of French morale, if these were sent and lost Britain would be totally defenceless against the *Luftwaffe* after France fell. The issue is still debatable and was coloured at the time by the fact that the French units, with the exception of General de Gaulle's tank forces in Artois, did not seem to be fighting with any great resolve or tenacity against the German invader. Britain had just 10 divisions in France compared with 103 French divisions but, *pro rata,* the British in the north were doing a great deal more fighting. The terrible French losses at Verdun in 1916 – over one million men were lost in that ten-month battle – were now taking a belated toll on French resolve, and without resolve the battle of France was indeed lost.

With the benefit of hindsight it is easy to see that even the full commitment of the RAF to France would not have made a great deal of difference and might well have led to the subsequent collapse of Britain. Even as it was, the BEF's position in Northern France had been fatally undermined by the collapse and surrender of Belgium on 15 May, a collapse that fully exposed the BEF's flank to the enemy's advance.

Nevertheless, British support of France continued, not least with a proposal from Churchill that the two countries should form an alliance and share citizenship – a rather quixotic suggestion at such a time. Churchill flew to France six times in the month up to the middle of June, each visit marking another decline in France's powers of resistance. A final spasm was the Weygand Plan at the end of May, a proposal from General Weygand that the British and the French First Army should strike south from the north and another French force would strike from the east, both attempting to cut off the powerful German thrust aiming at Paris and the Seine. This plan came to nothing, for the French forces along the Maginot Line failed to move and the British attack around Arras and St Quentin, on the old Great War battlefields, encountered the full force of *panzers* and *Stukas* and rapidly came to a halt.

With that reverse, General Gott, the BEF commander, saw no option but a steady withdrawal to the Channel coast and the evacuation of British forces to England before they could be rounded up by the Germans. By 24 May the Germans had pushed the BEF, some 350,000 men, back to the coast and into a heavily bombed pocket around Dunkirk. This withdrawal to a shrinking perimeter led to the epic of the Dunkirk evacuation – Operation DYNAMO – four tense days between 27 May and 1 June.

During those tense days the entire attention of the British people focussed on the shrinking Dunkirk perimeter and the exploits of the 'Little Ships', an armada of civilian yachts, pleasure steamers, lifeboats and shallow draft coastal craft, manned by civilians, naval reservists or cadets, that sailed across the Channel, lifted some 350,000 British and French troops off the Dunkirk beaches and brought them safely home, though most of their transport and equipment had to be left behind

There is a good deal of myth on both sides of the Atlantic surrounding the epic of Dunkirk. Royal Navy destroyers operating from the quays of Calais and Dunkirk actually rescued more men than the 'Little Ships' removed from the beaches, but the actions of Dunkirk were a chance for the public to help, for civilians to do something positive, to rally the nation. As a result, when the total of men evacuated was totted-up and made known, morale in Britain soared.

In the decades since 1940 many American historians have referred to the Dunkirk evacuation as a 'humiliation' for the British people, citing Dunkirk as a defeat that coloured British attitudes for the rest of the war. It is hard to find evidence in support of this conclusion. Dunkirk was certainly a defeat and a serious one but the British people did not feel humiliated, at the time or since.

Quite the contrary: the Dunkirk evacuation was greeted with joy and jubilation and a great sense of relief, even euphoria, not only in getting their troops back but also in being free from the entanglement of Allies. The British were on their own, with their backs to the wall, and generally they preferred it that way. Indeed, so exhilarated were the British in the days after Dunkirk that on 4 June, two days after the end of the evacuation, Churchill found it necessary to issue a word of caution to the people via another statement in the House of Commons; *'We must be careful not to attribute to this event the attributes of victory,'* he stated, *'wars are not won by evacuations.'*

This comment was perfectly true but it did little to halt the general joy among the population. The British were now alone; Western Europe was in enemy hands and the Empire at large had yet to muster – although Australian, South African, New Zealand and Canadian pilots were now manning aircraft in Fighter Command, a Command that was shortly to contain two squadrons – the Eagle Squadrons – of American volunteers. The *Wehrmacht* was twenty miles from the white cliffs of Dover, the *Luftwaffe* were moving onto recently captured airfields in France and Holland, ready to renew their offensive, and the U-boats had now acquired good ports on the Atlantic coast. Hitler and his generals were awaiting Britain's seemingly inevitable surrender while planning the invasion of Britain *Operation Seelowe* (Operation Sealion), in case Churchill and his people refused to see sense.

The nation was rallied on 4 June by yet another of Churchill's speeches, summing-up again the spirit of the people:

'Even though large tracts of Europe and many old and famous states have fallen or may fall into the grip of the Gestapo and all the odious apparatus of Nazi rule, we shall not flag or fail. We shall go on to the end. We shall fight in France, we shall fight on the seas and oceans, we shall fight with growing confidence and strength in the air, we shall defend our island, whatever the cost may be.'

'We shall fight on the beaches, we shall fight on the landing grounds, we shall fight in the streets and in the hills; we shall never surrender. And even if, which I do not for one moment believe, this island or a large part of it was subjugated and starving, then our Empire beyond the seas, armed and guarded by the British Fleet, would carry on the struggle until in God's good time the new world with all its power and might, steps forth to the liberation of the old.'

France had not yet finally surrendered when this speech was made; many of the French soldiers lifted from Dunkirk were shipped back to the Breton ports or Bordeaux. British units were still defending Calais and fighting alongside the French south and west of Paris, which fell on 14 June. The French Government finally gave in on 16 June when Marshal Petain took over the burden of office and started surrender talks with Germany, signing the instrument of surrender in that same railway carriage at Compiegne in which the Germans had been obliged to sign the armistice agreement in November 1918.

Two days after this sad event, Churchill brought bleak news to the House of Commons:

'The Battle of France is over. I expect that the Battle of Britain will shortly begin. Upon this battle depends the survival of Christian civilization. Upon it depends our own British life and the long continuity of our institutions and our Empire.'

'The whole fury and might of the enemy must very soon be turned upon us. Hitler knows that he will have to break us in this island or lose the war. If we can stand up to him, all Europe will be free, and the life of the world will move forward into broad sunlit uplands. But if we fail then the whole world, including the United States, and all that we have known and cared for, will sink into the abyss of a new dark age, made more sinister and perhaps more prolonged by the lights of perverted science.'

'Let us therefore brace ourselves to our duty and so bear ourselves that if the British Commonwealth and Empire last for a thousand years men will still say, "This was their finest hour."'

This speech is typically Churchillian, but again the words lose a great deal without the voice. The speech contains hard facts, blunt forecasts and, in the penultimate paragraph, a nudge to the United States that even 3,000 miles of turbulent ocean would not be a broad enough moat for the hard times that were coming. Finally, there is that ringing appeal, straight to the heart of the British people, that if everyone did their duty without flinching all would yet be well – and if they failed then they should go down honourably in battle and their sacrifice would be remembered.

This pending German invasion required calculation on both sides. Britain had last been invaded by William of Normandy in 1066; the British Navy had thwarted all subsequent attempts. That was still a possibility but things were different now. The Royal Navy were no longer in total control of the Narrow Seas. The Royal Navy could certainly dominate the Channel but the *Luftwaffe* could quickly sink any Royal Navy ships that ventured on those narrow waters, provided they could gain air superiority over the Channel.

This put the onus for defending Britain on some 1,200 young men, the trained fighter pilots of RAF Fighter Command. If they could keep control of the skies, while the Army reformed and re-equipped, an invasion of Britain could not take place. These pilots – the famous, now legendary '*Few*' – were the last bulwark of Britain in the Spitfire Summer of 1940.

The Germans also knew this. The first stage in the invasion of Britain must be to destroy the RAF and the *Luftwaffe*, which had already overwhelmed the air forces of Poland, Holland, Belgium and France had no doubt that they could do this. They had well-trained and very experienced crews, excellent fighters in the *Me-109* and *Me-110* and plenty of them, plus a great quantity of bombers to shatter British cities and bomb RAF airfields. By August the *Luftwaffe* had 2,699 operational aircraft in France, including 1,000 bombers and over 900 fighters; the RAF could muster about 600 fighters in 49 squadrons and around a thousand pilots. Apart from in the Spitfire squadrons RAF Fighter Command would be outmatched and outnumbered and, according to Herman Goering, the commander of the German *Luftwaffe*, the issue would shortly be settled. It was not to work out like that.

The British had a secret weapon – radar – and excellent fighter control centres all round the coast. These centres were able to spot the build-up of German formations as soon as they took off and send the fighter squadrons up to meet the enemy as they came across the British coast. There were never enough British fighters but they were always there – the *Luftwaffe,* try as it might, could not drive the RAF from the skies. Blue summer skies full of vapour trails and the sight of a dozen or twenty Spitfires and Hurricanes diving down to take on a hundred or two hundred German aircraft – and knocking a proportion out of the sky – remains an enduring memory for those who stood in the streets and fields of England and saw the Battle of Britain fought out overhead that summer.

The Battle of Britain began as soon as the Dunkirk evacuation ended with attacks on Channel shipping and went on throughout July and August, with daylight raids on London and the South Coast ports, the onslaught spreading gradually to the Midlands and the North of England.

The Battle of Britain lasted until the end of September. During those months there were air battles every day and given the odds, the RAF did well to hold its own. The pilots took off six to eight times a day to engage the enemy formations, the Hurricanes engaging the bombers, the more agile Spitfires taking on the German fighters. Losses were high; between 24 August and 6 September, to give one example, the RAF lost 106 pilots killed and 128 seriously wounded and a total of 466 Spitfires or Hurricanes destroyed or badly damaged.

These losses represented about a quarter of the pilots with which the RAF had entered the battle, and by the end of August a shortage of pilots was more worrying than a shortage of fighters. The problem of replacing pilots and aircraft was only one worry – the Germans had now switched their attacks from London and the towns and cities to the fighter airfields and to the radar stations that provided the fighter controllers with so much vital information.

The crux of the Battle of Britain came on 15 September, 1940, when the *Luftwaffe* made its largest raid on London, an event watched by Churchill from the Control Room of No. II Group, Fighter Command, at Uxbridge, just west of London. The battle went on all day with constant reports of '20 plus,' '40 plus,' '60 plus' German aircraft, coming in to attack and bomb. As they came the RAF fighter squadrons went up to meet them until by mid-afternoon there were only 5 RAF squadrons left in reserve. By early evening all were committed – already either in the air or on the ground, re-arming, getting ready to take off again. And then, gradually, as the evening turned to night the enemy tide receded – the *Luftwaffe* limped back to France, leaving 56 aircraft smoking in the fields of Kent and many others on the bed of the English Channel. Two days later Hitler postponed Operation Sealion until the spring of 1941. The Battle of Britain was over and the British had won it.

It had been a near-run thing. When the final scores were totted up, the RAF had lost 915 aircraft; the *Luftwaffe*, 1,733 – this last figure according to German records. Numbers had not prevailed against guts and tenacity and Churchill's House of Commons tribute to the RAF fighter pilots was most richly deserved:

> *'The gratitude of every home in our island, in our Empire and indeed, throughout the world, except in the abodes of the guilty, goes out to the British airmen who, undaunted by odds, unwearied in their constant challenge and mortal danger, are turning the tide of war by their prowess and by their devotion. Never in the field of human conflict was so much owed by so many to so few.'*

The British were not given long to enjoy this victory. Another battle was beginning, one much longer and much harder on the civilian population; now the many must follow the example of the Few.

In 1939 RAF Bomber Command, which had been active throughout the Battle of Britain attacking German invasion barges in the Channel ports, had learned that daylight bombing was prohibitively expensive. The squadrons had recorded losses of up to 50 percent on some operations and Bomber Command had therefore switched to night bombing, which was far less accurate and not much safer.

The *Luftwaffe* had also learned that daylight operations were costly and it too switched to night attacks, but they had one great advantage over the RAF. To reach the Ruhr, British bombers must make a flight of some 300 miles. To reach and bomb London from an airfield in France required the Germans to fly barely eighty miles – and the river Thames provided the perfect pathway, glittering in the moonlight, from the Channel to the centre of the target. On 4 September, 1940, Hitler had declared that he would 'erase' British cities from the map and at the end of September, the night bombing of British cities – the German *Blitz* – began in earnest.

Between 7 September and 3 November, an average of 200 German bombers attacked London every night. They destroyed the London docks and the City of London and large areas in the east of the City; mile after mile of London was reduced to rubble. Bombs also rained down on other parts of the city suburbs, and on many other towns and cities – ports like Liverpool and Southampton, inland towns like Coventry. Coventry suffered a terrible nightlong attack on 14 November, when 500 German aircraft attacked the town; over 400 people were killed, thousands more were injured and the entire town centre was gutted.

The Blitz went on, night after night, throughout the autumn and winter and well into the spring of 1941 and only ended when, abandoning all plans for Operation Sealion, Hitler sent the *Luftwaffe* east for the attack on Russia in the summer of 1941 (codename *Operation Barbarossa*). Before it ended, the *blitz* had killed 60,000 British civilians and done great damage, shattering many towns and cities, not all of them military targets – cathedral towns like Canterbury, York and Exeter were also attacked.

The Blitz did not, however, shatter the morale of the British people, or their dauntless Prime Minister. '*Britain can take it*' was the popular comment and life went on. Every morning the people would emerge from their shelters – many Londoners spent their nights on the platforms of the Underground stations – and, having swept up the broken glass, or surveyed the wreck of their homes, went back to work in the offices, shops or war factories.

There was not a lot Churchill could do to stop these raids – the night fighters were not numerous or equipped with suitable aids and the anti-aircraft guns and barrage balloons could do little to mitigate these night attacks. Nevertheless, there was the morale factor; heavy guns were positioned in the London parks and ordered to blaze away into the night sky, cheered on by a public anxious to hit back. Air Marshal Sir Arthur Harris – Bomber Harris – from February 1942 the commander of RAF Bomber Command, spoke for many when he viewed the fires raging around St Paul's cathedral and said that the Germans were *'sowing the wind and would reap the whirlwind.'*

Elsewhere, for a while, matters were going better. Anticipating the fall of France and, like Soviet Russia in 1939, anxious for a share of the resulting spoils, Italy had entered the war on the side of Germany, invading the South of France and sending an Army from Libya into Egypt. This proved Mussolini's greatest mistake. The Italian invasion of Egypt was met by General Sir Richard O'Connor's small force, the two-division strong Western Desert Force, and was soundly trounced in a number of engagements.

This first Western Desert campaign culminated in the total destruction of the Italian Army at Beda Fomm at the end of 1940; more than 130,000 Italian soldiers entered British POW camps and the Italian Army in North Africa was totally destroyed. This defeat obliged the Germans to send support to their Italian allies in Greece and North Africa so General Erwin Rommel – the *Desert Fox* – was sent to Tripoli with the first elements of what became the *Afrika Korps*. Malta, the island fortress of the Mediterranean and a bastion for the British Mediterranean Fleet, was besieged and bombed relentlessly; the air attacks on Malta would continue until the Allied invasion of Sicily in 1943, but the island fortress of Malta did not fall.

At sea the submarine war continued, with constant monthly losses to the Merchant Navy from the wide-ranging wolf packs of the German U-boat fleet. Nor was it just submarines; surface raiders like the *Hipper* and the *Scheer* also took their toll of British convoys. Writing to President Roosevelt in December 1940, Churchill stated that in the five weeks up to 3 November, 420,300 tons of shipping had been lost, and there now was the growing problem of finance.

Until November 1940 Britain had paid cash for everything received: food, weaponry, fuel – over $4.5 billion and now only $2 billion were left in the Treasury. A further sum of $300 million in shares taken over from private investors had also been sold off, but even the sale of Britain's gold reserves would not fund the struggle for long. Britain's gold reserves had been sent to the US and would soon be used up, but in December 1940 President Roosevelt introduced the Lend-Lease Act. Under Lend-Lease the US would produce and pay for the weapons of war – especially shipping – and lease them to Britain for the duration of the war.

Roosevelt introduced this Act to the US Congress and public in simple terms: *'Suppose my neighbour's house is on fire? I have a hose and if he connects my hose to his hydrant he can put out the fire. Say that hose cost me 15 dollars. I don't say to him, "Neighbour, I want 15 dollars for the use of that hose." – I want the hose back after the fire is over.'*

Churchill put the situation another way – *'Give us the tools and we will finish the job'* – but tools alone would not be enough. Britain needed allies. The US was proving a good friend but was as yet unwilling to enter the war. The Empire had mustered but needed training and weapons, and Japan was hovering, waiting for the moment to strike. The British Empire needed some major ally, some nation to share the burden of this growing struggle with the Axis powers.

In the summer of 1941, this ally came – from a most surprising quarter and largely thanks to the German *Führer*, Adolph Hitler. In June 1941, Hitler sent his panzers to attack Soviet Russia, his former ally in the rape of Poland. And so, thanks to this massive German miscalculation, Britain acquired her first major ally in the Second World War.

10. Barbarossa to Overlord

1941 - 1944

'He mobilised the English language and sent it into battle.'

President John F. Kennedy,
on granting US citizenship to Churchill, 1963

Although the German attack on Russia – Operation *Barbarossa* – in June 1941 brought the Soviets into the war on Britain's side, the advent of Russia did not ease the burden on Britain. Quite the contrary; the fact that the Soviet Union had sided with Germany since August 1939 and shared the spoils of Hitler's eastern conquests did not embarrass the Soviet leader, Marshal Josef Stalin, in the slightest. He was now Britain's ally and he expected British aid.

Stalin immediately demanded the shipping of military supplies from Britain and an invasion of Europe – a Second Front – as soon as possible, to take the pressure off the Red Armies, currently falling back before the German onslaught. Churchill hastened to oblige, telling those who objected to this instant support of Russia that *'if Hitler invaded hell I should make a favourable reference to Satan in the House of Commons.'*

The problem was that Britain's military capacity was already overstretched. The tanks, guns, trucks, fuel and food sent to Russia had to be taken away from the scanty supplies earmarked for the Middle East, where the British Eighth Army was currently locked in a closely fought struggle with General Erwin Rommel's *Panzerarmee Afrika*, in a campaign that was to sway up and down the North African coast for the next year and a half.

Nevertheless, Russia had to be supported and off went the supplies, fought across the North Sea and the Arctic Ocean by the Royal Navy, to the Russian ports of Archangel and Murmansk. Churchill also took to the waves, sailing in the battleship *Prince of Wales* to meet President Roosevelt at Placentia Bay in Newfoundland, a meeting that took place on 10-11 August and had some unforeseen consequences for Churchill and the British people.

The meeting was called to discuss the present state of relations between the two countries but Roosevelt began by suggesting that, *'they should draw up a joint declaration, laying down the broad principles which should guide our policies along the same road.'* The resulting document was the Atlantic Charter and its effects were to be far reaching.

The Atlantic Charter is quite short and the final draft – the Joint Declaration – contains just eight clauses, of which two became highly controversial. The Third Clause stated that the signatories, *'Respect the rights of all people to choose the form of government under which they will live.'* The Fourth Clause stated that, *'They will strive to bring about a fair and equitable distribution of essential produce, not only within their territorial boundaries but also between the nations of the world'.*

These clauses may seem unexceptional today but they were subject to a varying interpretation at the time and caused problems later. Churchill saw the Third Clause as a simple declaration of their joint resolve to end Nazi tyranny; Roosevelt saw it as a lever with which to destroy the British Empire by prising the colonies from British control.

As for the Fourth Clause, this was seen in the US as British acceptance of the American demand for an end to Imperial Preference, the trade links that bound the British Empire together that would open them up to US commerce. No dispute arose over these clauses at the time but it did not take long before the US interpretation was put in train, and eventually proved highly successful. The British Empire duly disappeared shortly after the end of the war; whether its departure has been of any benefit to the United States or the world at large is quite another matter.

Churchill returned to the UK and further demands for action on the Western Front and a landing on the coast of France or the Low Countries from Mr Maisky, the Soviet Ambassador, who *'emphasised in bitter terms how for the last eleven weeks Russia had been bearing the brunt of the German onslaught virtually alone.'*

Bearing in mind that Britain had been bearing the brunt of German attacks alone for the last two years, Churchill's reply was restrained:

' Remember' he told Maisky, *'that only four months ago we in this Island did not know whether or not you were coming in against us on the German side. Indeed, we thought it quite likely that you would. Even then we felt sure we would win in the end. We never thought our survival was dependent on your action either way. Whatever happens, and whatever you do, you of all people have no right to make reproaches to us.' 'Thereafter',* said Churchill, *'the Ambassador's tone perceptibly changed.'*

This discussion taught Churchill a useful lesson; placating the Russians did not work. It was necessary to stand up to them in debate, dismiss their arguments, and not allow them to get away with any of their outrageous demands. Politeness was wasted on tyrants.

So the war continued for the British, in North Africa, the North Atlantic, and the skies over Germany, while the Germans and Russians fought before Moscow. Then, three months later, on 7 December, 1941, the war expanded yet again when the Japanese attacked the base of the US Pacific Fleet at Pearl Harbor in Hawaii and the United States entered the war.

Although it took the Japanese attack on Pearl Harbor to get the United States off the fence, and Hitler's declaration of war on America to expand the US response to Europe, the US had been supporting Britain against Fascism from quite early days with food and munitions, all in return for prompt cash payments, and then with credit facilities – Lend-Lease – and latterly with anti-submarine patrols in the Western Atlantic. That was as far as President Roosevelt was able to go without full Congressional approval, which was not forthcoming.

Not every American gave whole-hearted support to Britain's struggle with Germany. Apart from the large and vocal Jewish community who were understandably outraged by the racist policies of Nazi Germany, many Americans felt that this European war was simply not their fight. Isolationism had been a factor in US politics since the 1920's, and the vast majority of US citizens, quite understandably, had no wish to be dragged into a European War – and certainly not on the side of Britain – the current notion in the US that America entered the war 'to save British butts' is refuted by these facts. Had Hitler not been unwise enough to declare war on the United States a week after Pearl Harbor, the US might have concentrated her strength against Imperial Japan.

Not all were even neutral in this matter; Anglophobia was and is rife in certain US circles. The German-Amerika Bund and American heroes like Charles Lindbergh were as active and vocal in support of Nazi Germany as the Jews were against it, while the Italian community and the Irish-Americans were adamant in their opposition to Britain; the fact that 80,000 Irishmen from the 'Old Country,' the equally neutral Irish Free State, had enlisted in the British Army did not dent this Celtic conviction. The support for Britain came from a mass of ordinary Americans rather than particular ethnic groups; hundreds of US citizens had already crossed the border into Canada to enlist in the RAF or the RCAF and US flying schools in Florida and Arizona were actively training British pilots and navigators from as early as 1940.

Private action apart, American isolationism was a powerful political message; Europe, after all, was a long way away. Besides, unlike the British, the Germans had never been enemies of the United States. Britain had been the oppressor in 1776, the enemy in 1812, and the unfriendly neutral in the US Civil War. Worst of all, Britain was an unrepentant *Imperial* power, keeping large areas of the world in colonial subjection. Added to that was the well-known fact that the British were a race of snotty-nosed, arrogant, class-ridden, effete, lazy incompetents who tended to sneer at hard-working Americans and were not worthy of support.

There is a considerable measure of cant in this summation. American history was not free from imperialism, as the 19th century annexations of Texas, New Mexico, California and the Philippines – and the enforcement of the Monroe Doctrine – bears witness, but speaking out against this mixture of myth and misconception was not an easy thing for any American President to do. Then came Pearl Harbor and suddenly Britain and the United States were allies.

The practical side of this military alliance was confirmed later in December at the Arcadia Conference in Washington, which took two steps that proved of vital importance in the conduct of the war and achieving the eventual victory. The first was the setting up of the Combined Chiefs of Staff Committee (CCS), composed of the US Joint Chiefs of Staff (the commanders of the US Army, Navy and Army Air Corps), and the British Chiefs of Staff. The CCS would handle the strategic conduct of the war under the direction of the US President, Franklin D. Roosevelt and the British Prime Minister, Winston Churchill, who would construct their policy after a series of meetings with the Russian leader, Marshal Josef Stalin – these leaders being generally known as The Big Three.

The second decision taken at Arcadia was for 'Germany First,' that the first task of the Allied forces would be the defeat of Nazi Germany. This was in line with the well-established article of strategic doctrine that when faced with an array of enemies – in this case Germany, Italy and Japan – the strongest, Germany, would be defeated first.

This decision was not reached without a certain amount of anguish in Washington. Japan had launched an infamous attack on US territory and there was a natural desire for retaliation and revenge. There was also the worry that if the Japanese were allowed to consolidate their gains in South East Asia and the Pacific they would be hard to dislodge.

The Japanese had not only attacked Pearl Harbor on 7 December. British territory in the Far East and other US territories in the Pacific had also been attacked and the Japanese armies were currently surging across the Phillipines, Burma, Malaya, Singapore and Hong Kong; if they were not stopped soon their eventual eviction would take much longer and be more costly. Admiral Ernest King, head of the US Navy and a member of the CCS – and a fervent Anglophobe – was particularly concerned on this point but was over-ruled by President Roosevelt and the chairman of the CCS, General George Marshall – the US would go for Germany first.

There was however, a small US caveat over the 'Germany First' decision, which was accepted by the Americans on the understanding that the direct attack on Germany would be made as soon as possible. A chronic argument then developed between Britain and the US on just how soon that possibility would be realised with a landing in France and an advance on Germany.

In December 1941, General Marshall was of the opinion that an assault on Western Europe could be launched within a few months, certainly not later than the summer of 1942. This was only some six months after the United States entered the war, but Marshall thought that this first attack, Operation SLEDGEHAMMER, should take the form of a cross-Channel assault to seize the Cotentin peninsula and the vital port of Cherbourg. That territory would be held for some months while more forces were brought across from the UK and the US after which the Allies would break out, surge across France and into Germany, and win the war. What the as-yet-undefeated *Wehrmacht* and *Luftwaffe* would be doing during this time was not apparently factored into this plan.

The British Chiefs of Staff, with rather more experience of fighting the German Army, were more sanguine about SLEDGEHAMMER, or at least about how soon that essential cross-Channel step could be successfully accomplished. Their view was that a cross-Channel invasion, while essential, could not be successfully launched until German power had been substantially stretched and much reduced, not only in the field with the writing down of the German Armies in Africa and Russia but also by sustained aerial bombardment of the industrial base supporting those armies in Germany. It would also be necessary to build up a powerful fleet of amphibious ships, and defeat the U-boat menace in the North Atlantic so that the vast US armies could be safely shipped to Britain.

This view prevailed, at least for 1942. Given the massive effort needed to carry out the D-Day landings in 1944, this was the right decision. Operation SLEDGEHAMMER was abandoned in favour of two other Operations, GYMNAST, an Allied invasion of North Africa by a force of American and British troops and ROUNDUP, the progressive build-up of US forces in the UK for an invasion of Europe in 1943. GYMNAST subsequently became Operation TORCH – the Allied landings in Morocco and Algeria under General Dwight D. Eisenhower, which took place in November 1942.

This brief outline of forthcoming Allied strategy and the varying attitudes between the British and their American ally is important. It will underline many of the decisions that followed and help to make clear the thinking behind the various inter-allied disputes over strategy and the best way to win the war and ensure the subsequent peace, which will surface again at the Casablanca Conference in January 1943. With that much clear we can now return to Winston Churchill and his current preoccupation in the Spring of 1942, the war in North Africa and the Far East. In neither theatre was the war going well.

On the day after Pearl Harbor, the Japanese landed strong forces in the north of Malaya and in a lightning campaign drove the British, Indian, and Australian forces back to the island of Singapore, which fell in early February – a great shock to Churchill. This was followed by various reverses in North Africa where a skilful German commander, Erwin Rommel, was still running rings round the British Eighth Army. Driven back from Tobruk in the Sidi Rezegh offensive of November and December 1941 – Operation CRUSADER – Rommel counter attacked in the spring of 1942 at Gazala, drove the British back pell-mell to the Alamein line and took the fortress of Tobruk, another crushing blow for the British Prime Minister.

Tobruk had held out against Rommel for eight months in 1941 and in the process had become a symbol to the British and Australian people; its loss after just one day in 1942 was an emotional setback, made all the worse for Churchill because the news arrived when the Prime Minister was in Washington, dining with President Roosevelt at the White House. An aide brought in the telegram and handed it to the President who read it briefly and passed it to Churchill. It said, '*Tobruk has surrendered with the loss of 25,000 men.*' Churchill records this as '*one of the heaviest blows I can recall during the war,*' a blow made even heavier by the previous loss of Singapore.

'*I did not attempt to hide from the President the shock I had received. It was a bitter moment. Defeat is one thing; disgrace is another. Nothing could exceed the sympathy and chivalry of my two friends* (General Ismay was with Churchill). *There were no re-proaches; not an unkind word was spoken. "What can we do to help?" asked Roosevelt.*'

Churchill asked that the Americans round up as many Sherman tanks as they could spare and ship them at once to the Middle East – and 300 Sherman tanks and 100 self-propelled guns were promptly despatched to Egypt.

The fall of Tobruk caused more than military problems for Churchill. The series of defeats suffered by the British since Rommel arrived in 1941 continued into the Spring of 1942 and raised serious questions about Churchill's entire strategy and the conduct of the war. It has to be said that many of the problems affecting the British Army in North

Africa were the result of decisions taken by Winston Churchill, both in failing to appreciate the very real problems facing the field commanders, Generals Wavell and Auchinleck, failing to divide a command that was already too big, and ordering them to take on extra tasks as well as countering the Axis armies in North Africa.

These included assistance to the Greeks, holding Crete, attacking the Italians in Abysinnia and the Vichy French in Syria – all without providing the necessary resources. These resources were, of course, in short supply, but if a shortage of resources led to failure the generals could not be exclusively blamed. Apart from being Prime Minister, Churchill was also War Minister so all the problems affecting the armies could be laid at his door and led to a censure motion in the House of Commons on 25 June, 1942:

> 'That this House, while paying tribute to the heroism and endurance of the Armed Forces of the Crown in circumstances of exceptional difficulty, has no confidence in the central direction of the war.'

This was a Vote of Confidence; if a Minister or a Government loses such a Vote it must resign. The debate on this motion took place on 1-2nd June, 1942 and led to some heated exchanges but when the censure motion was put to the Members it was thrown out by 475 votes to 25.

Nevertheless, it had been a shot across Churchill's bow and he took heed of the warning. Something had to be done about the British command structure in the Middle East and the only one able to make changes was the Defence Minister. Churchill flew to Cairo and made a tour of the troops, inspecting their equipment and the defences of the Alamein Line where Rommel's advance from Gazala had been brought to a halt.

Eighth Army was short of trained soldiers and lacked guns and tanks – and the tanks and guns it had were inferior to those possessed by the German-Italian force, the *Panzerarmee Afrika*. However, the catalyst in all this was the capability of General Rommel; until the

British could find a general who could cope with Rommel little would be achieved.

The current British commander in the Middle East was General Claude Auchinleck, who had taken direct command of Eighth Army and stopped Rommel's advance. However, the various defeats of 1941-42 and the loss of Tobruk had undermined his position and Churchill decided that Auchinleck must go. Various officers were considered but the man chosen was a small, peppery general with no desert experience, Lt-General Sir Bernard Law Montgomery, a man known to his friends, and his much more numerous enemies, as Monty.

In August 1942, Montgomery replaced Auchinleck as commander of Eighth Army, with General Sir Harold Alexander as his Commander-in-Chief. A few weeks after taking up his command, Montgomery inflicted a defeat on Erwin Rommel at the battle of Alam Halfa, a considerable boost to Eighth Army's morale and to Montgomery's reputation.

Then, on the night of 23 October, 1942, Eighth Army attacked Rommel's forces at El Alamein and after twelve days of fighting among the minefields, drove the *Panzerarmee Afrika* back in full retreat. This retreat ended in May 1943 when the Allied Armies in North Africa – 18th Army Group, commanded by General Sir Harold Alexander, the British First and Eighth Armies and the US Second Corps under Patton – the whole under General Dwight Eisenhower, now the Supreme Allied Commander in the Mediterranean – forced the remnants of Rommel's forces to surrender at Tunis.

Churchill made two speeches in this period containing memorable phrases. Speaking at the Lord Mayor of London's Mansion House dinner on November 10 and referring to the Alamein victory he said, *'Now this is not the end. It is not even the beginning of the end. But it is, perhaps, the end of the beginning.'* Another part of this speech touched on the US interpretation of the Atlantic Charter: *'I have not become the King's First Minister'* growled Churchill, *'to preside over the destruction of the British Empire.'* In January 1943, after the fall of Tripoli to Eighth Army, he told the soldiers that *'When this war is over, it will be enough for a man to say "I marched and fought with the Desert Army"* and wept when the pipers of the 51ˢᵗ Highland Division, *'those wonderful fighting Jocks'* led the British infantry though the streets and out again to the battle.

US ground forces had entered the war against Germany with Operation TORCH – the invasion of Algeria and Morocco in November 1942. With the defeat of the German Armies in North Africa the next decision that had to be made was where should the Allies next apply their growing strength against the German military machine.

The decision on this point was taken at the Casablanca Conference in January 1943 and the final decision was for a landing in Sicily, to be followed with an invasion of the Italian mainland. Operation OVER-LORD, the Allied invasion of France, was to be delayed for another year but outline plans were to be laid by a small team under a British general, Sir Fredrick Morgan. Morgan's title was *Chief of Staff to the Supreme Allied Commander* and from these initials his subsequent proposals became known as the COSSAC plan.

At this point, dissension intervenes in the Allied leadership. With OVERLORD scheduled for 1944 what were their armies to do in the meanwhile? Churchill was in favour of an attack on Italy – a country he described as *'the soft underbelly of Europe,'* a description which the troops who fought in Italy over the next two years found wildly out of touch with the terrain. On the other hand the British Chiefs of Staff still thought it necessary to stretch the Axis powers as far as possible, and that with the U-boats as yet undefeated and the North African campaign not ended until May of 1943, it was clear that Italy was the best option for what was left of the campaigning season.

Sicily was duly invaded on 9-10 May, 1943 and in Alllied hands by 17 August. The fall of Sicily led to the downfall of Mussolini, who was dismissed from office and briefly imprisoned before being released by a German SS group. Two weeks after the capture of Sicily, on 3 September the British Eighth Army landed on the toe of the Italian mainland and a week later the Anglo-American Fifth Army landed at Salerno, just a few hours after the Italian Government capitulated.

The Italian surrender did not prove of great benefit to the Allied commanders in Italy. German forces occupied the country and the fighting for Italy went on until the end of the war, with great battles on the Rapido, at Cassino, and Anzio, for the Gothic Line and the Po Valley; it also signaled the beginning of a deep if polite dispute between Churchill and Roosevelt and their respective advisors.

It was now apparent to all that Germany was going to lose this war. The argument therefore, at least on Churchill's side, was about the political shape of post-war Europe and the growing possibility that Nazi domination would be replaced by Communist domination, certainly of the Balkans and large parts of Central Europe. One way to prevent this, Churchill argued, was to push up the Italian peninsula as fast as possible and get onto the Hungarian plains or into Austria before the Red Army arrived.

Roosevelt and his advisors did not agree. The President had no intention of getting involved in European affairs – that would be left to the Europeans and a new organization the United Nations – nor was he interested in what his advisers described as 'Balkan adventures.' These were widely believed, at least in Washington, to be yet another example of Churchill's engrained imperialism. The Soviets, whatever their faults, were at least republicans and Roosevelt fully intended to bring all the US troops back home within two years of the end of the war.

Another effect of Churchill's pleading for advances in Northern Italy was a growing conviction among the Joint Chiefs and in Washington that Churchill was trying to wriggle out of the OVERLORD commitment. This was not so, but a conviction, once arrived at, is a hard thing to dislodge.

That Churchill was quite right in his estimation of Russian intentions was borne out by the 50 years of Cold War with the Soviets that followed the defeat of Germany in 1945, and the fact that, even today, sixty years after the war ended, there are still tens of thousands of US troops in Europe. That did not matter at the time; the US commanders were determined not to get involved in operations outside Italy and were able to curb any contrary intentions, including those of their own commanders in that theatre, by constantly reducing the number of US divisions in Italy and refusing to provide an adequate number of amphibious vessels for flanking operations.

Churchill also used up a certain amount of political credibility and a great deal of American patience in 1943 and early 1944 by harping on the possibility of luring Turkey into the war, which, he claimed, would have great benefits for the Allied cause and would spread alarm and despondency among German forces in the Balkans. This may well have been true but such a proposal came a little late, and flew in the face of the hard fact that Turkey had no intention whatsoever of joining the war at all.

These arguments over the Italian-Balkan strategy crystallised in the summer of 1944 in the dispute over Operation ANVIL, later Operation DRAGOON, and Allied landing, largely with French forces on the Mediterranean coast of France, on or in close support of D-Day. In the event and largely due to a shortage of shipping, ANVIL/ DRAGOON had to be delayed until mid-August, but Churchill was very determined that it should be called off and the forces destined for that operation should be retained in Italy and used either to push west along the French Riviera or, better still, employed to break the defences of the Gothic Line, the last major defensive position in Italy and push on into Yugoslavia and Hungary. Once again though, special pleading was to no avail; Churchill's voice was no longer heard and his influence was declining as Britain's military contribution declined as a percentage of the Allied whole.

The main US worry was OVERLORD, the invasion of France. Any earlier belief that this invasion would be easy had long since disappeared – SLEDGEHAMMER was now seen as a distant delusion – and Eisenhower and Marshall were now very concerned that every man, tank, and gun available should be sent to Normandy and deployed on D-Day or during the subsequent campaign. Churchill fully supported OVERLORD – allegations that he was lukewarm to the invasion have no factual basis – but felt that the Italian campaign could aid OVER-LORD and offer significant political advantages in the post-war world.

'*There can be no doubt at all,*' he wrote later, '*that Italy was the greatest prize open to us at this stage, and provision for it could have been made without causing any delay to the main cross-Channel plan of 1944.*'

Nor was Churchill well at this time; his health was causing a great deal of anxiety to Clementine, his doctor, Lord Moran, and his advisors. Churchill was now 69 and still working very long hours, and fuelling his work with large amounts of whisky. This is not to say that Churchill was a drunk, only that he drank too much for his own good. In fact, throughout his life he seems to have displayed a great tolerance for hard liquor and champagne, both of which he consumed in considerable quantities without visible effect.

The greater risk was the constant strain and long hours he kept working. Although he still tended to take a nap of one or two hours in the afternoon, he would then summon his advisors and secretaries and work until two and three in the morning with a break for dinner and perhaps a film show – Churchill was a great movie buff and delighted in seeing all the latest movies in the small private cinema at Chequers, the Prime Ministerial country home. Even so, all this work took its toll and Churchill was to experience several bouts of ill health, at least one of them requiring a long rest in Marrakesh. Painting had not become his great relaxation and although Churchill was never willing to take time off from his duties, he could usually be persuaded to take a day or two off for painting.

Nor was all Churchill's time taken up with the war. Much as he preferred military matters he was the Prime Minister and also had a country to run. With victory in prospect if not actually in sight, post-war concerns were starting to appear in Britain. What was this war for? A better world was one answer but a better world for whom? There were plenty of people in Britain who remembered the promises of 1918, of 'a land fit for heroes' which had turned out to be one of unemployment and poor housing. There was a general determination that the soldiers were not to be cheated this time, and the broad aims for a post-war Britain were laid out at the end of 1942 in the Beveridge Report.

In early 1941, Sir William Beveridge, a civil servant, had been asked by the Trades Union Congress to write a report on the state of health insurance. Sir William duly set to work and it soon became apparent that his Report would cover a much wider field of public concerns. When it was published, in December 1942, the Report (CMD 6404) was an all-out attack, and a Plan for tackling, the five social evils of Want, Disease, Ignorance, Squalor and Idleness. These led to programmes for full employment, comprehensive education, the National Health Service, and other steps to a better future.

Beveridge laid down the principles of what later became the Welfare State and held that a nation that could find the money for all-out war must be able to fund a worthwhile society in peacetime. The Report proved immensely popular and promptly led to a public demand for 'Beveridge Now,' which Churchill felt obliged to resist.

Churchill was not against social provision; far from it. With Lloyd George he had pioneered social legislation measures like old age pensions and unemployment pay as long ago as 1908. His objections to Beveridge were on the grounds of timing – let us win the war first and then win the peace – and cost. He was by no means sure that the figures produced by Beveridge which showed how the Plan could be payed for were accurate, and in the end they proved to be wildly optimistic. Even so, public pressure was too strong and work to implement the Beveridge Plan got under way, but Churchill's lukewarm reception of Beveridge's proposals was not forgotten by the electorate.

Fortunately, there was soon another more pertinent distraction. On 6 June,1944, the Allied Armies went ashore on the northern coast of France – Operation OVERLORD, the long awaited invasion of Normandy, had begun.

11. Victory and Defeat

1944 - 1945

*'We are now entering a world of imponderables
and at every stage occasions for self-questioning arise.
Only one link in the chain of destiny can be handled at a time.'*

Winston S. Churchill,
House of Commons, 27 February, 1945

The Allied Armies landed in Normandy on 6 June, 1944 – a date that will be forever known as 'D-Day' although every military operation, large or small, has a D-Day, marking the day on which a battle begins. Churchill had intended to accompany the invasion fleet to the beaches and was only dissuaded from this course of action by a personal plea from King George VI, who badly wanted to go himself.

Churchill managed to get across the Channel on 12 June, D plus 6, travelling in a destroyer and escorted by Admiral Sir Philip Vian. Once across, he went ashore to visit General Montgomery, who was currently commanding the Allied Armies in Normandy, stayed for lunch within the sound of the guns, and then re-embarked to sail up the coast and watch Allied warships pounding enemy positions ashore. Before the day ended he had persuaded Admiral Vian to move the destroyer closer to the coast shore and fire a few salvos against the enemy. Only then, having taken some part in the war against the enemy, was he ready to return to England.

Churchill returned frequently to the bridgehead thereafter, never happier than when among the troops or talking to the front line commanders – anywhere close to action. The campaign in Normandy was a grinding hard-fought battle, or series of battles, not without much subsequent controversy, but it ended in the last week of August with the total defeat of the German armies in Normandy and their expulsion across the Seine. This victory was achieved according to the strategic plan laid down before D-Day and well ahead of schedule, but this happy event was not without the now usual inter-allied squabbles.

Many of these wrangles, inevitably, involved General Sir Bernard Montgomery, to whom most of the US commanders were, to put it mildly, antipathetic, though it was 'Monty's' strategy that ensured the Normandy successes. On 1 September, 1944, the Allied Supreme Commander, General Dwight D. Eisenhower, took direct charge of ground operations, while retaining the post of Supreme Commander. This move had also been planned well before D-Day though whether it was wise in the event is still debated in military circles.

Shortly after the Normandy invasion, war returned to the Home Front with the start of the German rocket and flying-bomb offensive – V-1 flying bombs and V-2 rockets – which fell indiscriminately on London from early July and caused considerable destruction and loss of life, including 121 killed (50 of them civilians) by one V-1 alone which landed on the Guards Chapel in Knightsbridge barracks during Sunday morning service. These aerial attacks made a rapid advance up the French coast even more essential – since many of the V-1 launch sites were on that coast, but from early September the Allied campaign in North West Europe slowed, largely for logistical reasons, mainly a shortage of fuel and supply ports.

Churchill was also still firmly against ANVIL/DRAGOON, the invasion of the South of France which had now been put back to mid-August. Churchill was particularly incensed by the news that four French and three US divisions were to be removed from Italy for DRAGOON, thus ending any real hope of a successful push north from Rome to Florence, the Po Valley, and the Alps – Rome having fallen on 4 June.

Churchill and the British Chiefs pushed hard for an extension of the Italian campaign into Hungary and Austria but to no avail. Roosevelt was still obsessed with the need to avoid what he described as 'Balkan adventures' and told Churchill that this was an election year; he would never survive the slightest setback in Normandy if it were learned that US forces had been 'diverted' to the Balkans. Churchill pointed out, wearily, that this was not about the Balkans, which lay east of the Adriatic, but aimed purely at taking Istria and Trieste in the North of Italy and so threatening Austria, a Nazi stronghold and Hitler's birthplace which the Germans must defend.

All this pleading and Churchill's explanations of the strategic benefits of this move, certainly to the European nations, were to no avail. Roosevelt would not change his mind and the Italian campaign, with all its possibilities for the post-war shape of Europe, was allowed to drift. It was, says Martin Gilbert, *'a low ebb in the Anglo-American wartime relationship.'*

The roots of this disagreement – dispute is perhaps too strong a word – lie in three areas. First, a disagreement over war aims. Roosevelt's war aim was victory, the defeat of the Fascist powers, an end to the Allied Colonial powers (or at least to their Empires), and the setting up of the UN to handle subsequent problems. All this was achieved but the results of that achievement were not what the US President anticipated; there was a failure in strategic thinking.

If the Fascist powers were simply replaced by the Communist powers which had been allowed to overrun much of Europe, what was gained? If the destruction of the Colonial Empires led to the Third World, a vast region steeped in anarchy, corruption, war, starvation and genocide, what was gained? As for the setting up of the United Nations, important as this was, that did not mean the democratic nations could safely abandon any effort to protect their own interests or police their own frontiers.

Churchill knew all this; he had the statesman's ability to look beyond the next action and ask, 'What happens then?' Roosevelt also knew all this but he was a politician and was not greatly concerned with subsequent outcomes. The US was a long way from Europe and, unlike the other Allied powers, would emerge from this war immensely richer, undamaged, and the greatest power on earth. Nations do not have friends, they have interests – and neither Roosevelt nor America was interested in Churchill's problems.

An illustration of the growing Soviet problem was starting to appear in Poland with the advance of the Red Army towards Warsaw. There were now two Polish Governments-in-exile, one based in London, which was supported by the Polish troops serving with the Allied Armies in Italy and Normandy and the Polish Underground fighters in Warsaw – and the Communist-backed Polish Government in Moscow, which later became known as the 'Lublin Government' after it moved to that Polish city.

The struggle between these two 'Governments' had yet to come into the open. When it did there was no doubt that Stalin would back the Lublin delegates with whatever force was necessary while the British and Americans supported, weakly, a joint Government for Poland, pending the final outcome of free democratic post-war elections.

This process was hardly likely to appeal to Stalin who had already insisted that his 'support' for the Allies, which largely consisted of demanding their support for Soviet Russia, was dependent on Russia retaining all the territory seized from Poland during the Soviet invasion in 1939 when Russia was allied to Nazi Germany. If the Poles wanted more territory, Stalin argued, they should compensate themselves by seizing German land east of the Oder and Neisse rivers. There was a good strategic reason for Stalin's demands. Russia had always seen

Poland as the invader's gateway to Mother Russia and felt a strategic need to hold the keys of that gate. If that meant stamping on the Poles, so be it.

On 31 July, 1944, Stalin proceeded to destroy the Polish Underground Army in Warsaw. With the Red Army just 15 miles from the city, the Poles rose against the German garrison, hoping to free their city before the Russians arrived or at least assist in their own liberation. The Germans sent four and a half divisions into Warsaw, two of them SS Divisions. While these divisions destroyed the city and killed tens of thousands of Polish civilians, the Red Army halted on the Vistula, a few miles away and let it happen. In spite of Churchill's pleas, Stalin even refused to let British aircraft drop ammunition and supplies into the city. The Poles held out until the end of August before they were overwhelmed and the Red Army moved in to occupy a shattered city replete with corpses.

In mid-August, while all this was going on, Churchill flew to the Mediterranean to watch the DRAGOON landings, the Franco-American landings in the South of France on 14-15 August. While there Churchill became involved in another political problem – Greece.

The British had long enjoyed an interest in Greek independence, supporting Greek freedom at every opportunity, a policy dating back to the actions of Lord Byron in the early years of the 19th century. The latest independence crisis arose when the German garrisons were withdrawn from Greece during the summer of 1944 and the Greek Communist guerrillas, ELAS, never forward in fighting the Germans, began to make their bid for power. Determined to prevent this Communist takeover of a newly liberated country, Churchill ordered the despatch of a British force to Athens - not to take over the country but to shore up the Greek Government until it could muster forces to tackle the Communist challenge.

This commitment soon led to further arguments with the Americans, who felt that the Greeks should sort out their own problems and that Churchill was again playing the imperialist role. The fact that the Communists in Yugoslavia and Russia were arming the ELAS rebels and urging them to take over the country and impose a Communist regime, and that Britain had an equal right to assist the Greek Government, escaped Washington's notice.

Face-to-face meetings between Churchill and Roosevelt usually resolved such difficulties and Roosevelt suggested that the two should meet in Quebec, without Stalin, who was always very reluctant to move far from the Soviet Union, though Roosevelt, for some reason, was equally reluctant to visit London, in spite of frequent invitations. This second Quebec conference – the OCTAGON conference – took place between 11–15 September and included discussion of the Morgenthau Plan, a proposal from US Secretary of the Treasury Henry Morgenthau, that German industry should be destroyed and Germany converted to a pastoral economy after the war. This unrealistic concept was promptly rejected on both sides of the Atlantic but proved very valuable to the Nazi propaganda machine, which were able to tell the German people what would happen to them if the Allies won the war – they would be turned into shepherds.

Discussions also took place on the progress of the Anglo-American Manhattan Project, the building of the atomic bomb, which was then in progress with a target date of August 1945, and how British forces from Europe should be deployed in the Pacific when the European war ended. More important than any of this was a certain meeting of minds over the conduct of the war and the shape of post-war Europe.

Having seen Roosevelt, Churchill decided to visit Stalin, arriving in Moscow on 9 October. Among various issues, Churchill and Stalin agreed on the extent of their post-war influence in Eastern Europe. This would vary from country to country – in Yugoslavia and Hungary, 50-50, in Romania, 90 percent Russian, in Greece, 90 percent British. Whether Stalin would keep to these percentages would soon be made clear, although Churchill followed up this agreement with a letter to Stalin reaffirming his belief that *'every country should have the form of Government which its people desire* and that *no ideology should be imposed on any small state.'* Churchill then had discussions with representatives of both Polish Governments but no agreement was reached. Stalin's support for his creatures in the Lublin Government was now obvious and there was little scope for compromise.

Meanwhile, as the Allied armies in North West Europe and Italy fought on throughout the winter of 1944-45, problems were looming at home. It was now clear that peace, if not actually in sight, was now looming over the horizon. This being so, the Coalition Government that had handled the conduct of the war so far was starting to fragment; Party politics were starting to emerge again. In October Churchill told the House of Commons that while he would prefer that the Coalition continued into the post-war period and fought the problems of peace, that was a matter for the House. If the Labour Party wished to withdraw from the Coalition after the defeat of Germany, a General Election would be called and the former political system resume.

'The foundation of all democracy', Churchill declared, 'is that the people have a right to vote. To deprive them of that makes a mockery of all the high-sounding phrases that are so often used. At the bottom of all the tributes paid to democracy is the little man, walking into the voting booth with a pencil and making a mark on a piece of paper.'

The future make-up of the House of Commons was in some ways the least of Churchill's problems; with the war clearly coming to an end, problems were appearing on every side. The war had shaken the old order loose and various power-brokers were jockeying for new positions in the post-war world at home and abroad. One particular problem for Britain was Palestine, a territory mandated to Britain by the League of Nations after the Balfour Declaration had declared British support for the establishment of a Jewish homeland.

This suggestion had infuriated the Palestinian Arabs and a form of civil war had been raging in Palestine since long before 1939. Now, with growing evidence of the Holocaust and the prospect of massive Jewish immigration after the war, it was clear that the Palestine question – should the Zionists be allowed to set up a new State of Israel in the midst of the Arab Middle East? – could not be put off much longer. Though Britain's Mandate was due to run out in 1948, and the British Government was very anxious to be rid of it, this problem would be another of Britain's post-war woes and cause further problems with the US, which could not then accept that the Arab-Jewish dispute over Palestine had no solution acceptable to both parties.

Greece was an even more pressing problem. Civil war between the Communists and the Greek Government had now started and British troops had now been deployed, although Washington had prevented US landing ships taking British troops to Athens, even though the Russians were openly supporting the Communist guerrillas now attempting to take Athens over by force of arms. The British intention in Greece was to stamp out all forms of military coup and after a period of peace, urge the Greek Government to hold free elections with the Archbishop of Athens acting as Regent in the meanwhile. All in all, there was plenty to discuss when the Big Three met for their next major meeting at Yalta in the Crimea, a meeting that would see a major split between the British and Americans and hand much of Eastern Europe over to the Communists.

None of that mattered too much to President Franklin D. Roosevelt who was now working on an earlier agenda, one dating back to before the Atlantic Charter of 1941. A long-time opponent of the British Empire, Roosevelt believed that Empire equalled tyranny and that the Colonial Empires must go – and as quickly as possible. He was less worried by the slow extinction of the Eastern European countries by the Russians.

US attacks on colonial rule by Britain, France, and Holland were to continue and be extremely successful; by the early 1960s the British Empire had all but disappeared, the French were hanging on by their fingers in Indo-China, a country later better known as Vietnam, and the Dutch were rapidly leaving Indonesia. The results of that precipitate 'End of Empire' era were the Vietnam War and the establishment of dictators in Iraq and many other countries. The issue of the day was freedom, and it is perhaps worth pointing out that the much-maligned

British Empire had been transformed into over 30 free and independent nations a full decade before a black citizen in many parts of America was free to sit where he or she wanted in a hometown bus or coffee shop.

Apart from colonialism, the other issue was the growing threat from Communism to the European democracies. Since 1943, Churchill had gradually become convinced that the Soviets were not going to be content with driving the Germans from Russian soil. They were equally determined to follow the retreating Germans across Eastern Europe into the Reich and would keep on heading west until they were stopped.

Churchill was unable to put this point across, or get any action to stop this process, partly because of the need to maintain the Big Three alliance and partly because he could not enlist any support from the US. Here again the root cause was US anti-imperialism, and Churchill's declining influence.

By early 1945 Britain had become the junior partner in the Big Three Alliance. This was largely a matter of demographics – the US and Soviet Russia had more troops in the field – but also reflected the fact that Churchill's early lustre as the sole democratic bastion against Fascism had faded since 1940-41. The era of power politics was back and the adage that 'nations did not have friends, but interests' was becoming more true day-by-day.

In fairness to the US President, it has to be added that Roosevelt was ill at Yalta. He would die a few months later, in April 1945, but at Yalta there is some evidence of political naivete; Roosevelt believed he had more in common with Josef Stalin than with Winston Churchill and could both handle Stalin and reach firm, lasting agreements with the Soviets.

Whatever Stalin's faults – tyrant, butcher, mass murderer of the kulaks, organizer of the Great Terror, constructor of the *gulags*, former ally of Nazi Germany, future oppressor of Eastern Europe – at least Stalin was not a rabid, imperialist aristocrat Britisher like Winston Churchill. Roosevelt truly believed that he could get along with Stalin and so make deals with a major power for the peace and security of the world – after the power of Britain and the other European nations had been destroyed, either as a result of the war or in the immediate post-war future.

No man is more easily deceived by another than a man who has previously deceived himself. In spite of a growing body of evidence, including dire warnings on Soviet aims and post-war intentions from the US Ambassador in Moscow, Roosevelt continued to believe in Stalin's faith and good will to the moment of his death. Not until the Berlin blockade of 1947 and the start of the Cold War did these self-applied scales drop from American eyes. The Yalta Conference began on 4 February, 1945, lasted for eight full days, and was an unmitigated disaster for the West.

The Conference began with a proposal from Churchill that the Allied Armies in Italy should land in Yugoslavia and join up with the left flank of the advancing Red Army for a push into Austria. This was another attempt to revive Churchill's aim of decisive action in Italy and did not have a hope of success. Then Roosevelt, who had already refused to meet Churchill privately in case Stalin took offence, met Stalin in private and emerged to suggest that the coming peace should be made by the major powers without any consultation with the small ones, a suggestion to which Stalin, who had already been consulted on this point, eagerly agreed.

Not so, said Churchill, that is not acceptable. He argued that the smaller nations also had a right to be consulted on matters that affected their future – 'the eagle should permit the small birds to sing,' he added, standing his ground until the proposal was dropped.

The next issue was the partition of Germany between the powers in the post-war period. Churchill pressed successfully for the French to be given an Occupation Zone. Stalin agreed provided it came from part of the British or American sectors. Stalin was then pleased, and Churchill dismayed, by Roosevelt's comment that the US occupation of Germany would be limited to two years and the boys would be home by 1948. There are still 57,000 US troops in Germany in 2003.

Further discussions on 6 February covered the establishment of the United Nations, and the rejection of Stalin's suggestion that all the 'states' of the Soviet Union – Georgia, Uzbekistan, Kazakstan, and so on – should have a seat in the General Assembly. The Three did agree that the smaller Security Council would be the main debating area for the settlement of disputes rather than the General Assembly.

However, the contentious issue at Yalta, one surfacing all the time, was Poland. This dispute largely involved Britain and the USSR. President Roosevelt declared that he was not seriously interested in the Polish question, there being very few Poles in the US – adding that *'Poland had been a source of trouble for over 500 years.'* There were very few Poles in Britain either; the issue was one of principle, not political advantage. Britain had gone to war in 1939 to honour a pledge to Poland and was unwilling to see the defeat of the Nazis herald the triumph of Russian Communism.

Churchill rejected Stalin's claim that the Lublin Poles had any right to speak for the entire Polish nation, insisting that the Poles were entitled to free elections and that the decision on the extent of Polish territory should be decided after the war and not at Yalta. The problem was that Stalin's armies were already over-running Poland. Stalin had no intention of pulling them back and without support from the US, Churchill was powerless to influence the take-over of Poland by the Soviets or their Polish Communist puppets. The arguments over Poland went on for five days, ending when Stalin suddenly offered to hold free elections in Poland *'within a month'* and allowing the participation of the London Poles.

Other topics included reparations and the treatment of German war criminals. Russia wanted to remove the bulk of Germany's undamaged industrial plant to the Soviet Union and eventually did so; after the war it was said by the troops in the Occupation Zones that *'the Russians got the factories, the Americans got the scientists, the French got the women and the British got the rubble.'* On the subject of war criminals, Stalin proposed that 50,000 German leaders should simply be shot out of hand – at which suggestion Churchill walked out of the session, saying his country would never be party to such a proposal.

Stalin also requested that any Soviet prisoners of war released from German camps by the Western Allies should be sent back to Russia as quickly as possible, as should any Russian or Yugoslav soldiers found in German uniforms. The result of this proposal was the summary execution, sometimes after torture, or confinement to the living death of the gulags of tens of thousands of Russian or Yugoslav men and women, handed back to the Communists after the war as a result of this agreement at Yalta.

The Yalta summit ended on 14 February with the usual hopeful communiqué, including that promise on the holding of Polish elections to set up a Provisional Polish Government of National Unity. On his return to the UK, Churchill encountered considerable unease about the situation in Poland, from where reports were coming in about arrests and deportations by the Russians and even executions of some free Poles who had survived the Warsaw Rising. Churchill's concerns over Poland dominated all other matters as the European war inched to its conclusion in March and April 1945.

Churchill visited British and Canadian units fighting on the German border in March and spent some time with General Eisenhower at Versailles, returning to London on March 2 to hear that the Soviets had decided that only those Poles selected by the Lublin Government would be allowed to stand in the forthcoming elections – it had taken Stalin a little over two weeks to go back on his commitment to free elections.

Worse was to follow with the arrest in Poland of those London Poles who had trusted Stalin's good faith and returned home; thousands of these had now been rounded up and sent east to Soviet labour camps. This information was sent on to Washington but got little response; Roosevelt was dying and with the ending of the European War American thoughts were tuning to the Pacific rather than some quarrel in Central Europe.

On 28 March, Churchill stood on the banks of the Rhine near Wesel and watched the British Second Army and the US Ninth Army cross the river with an airborne and amphibious assault, an enjoyable interlude marred by further dire news from Poland – the fourteen Polish leaders from London who had gone home to contest the upcoming elections had been arrested on arrival and taken to a Soviet Army base. All Churchill's fears over Stalin's ruthless duplicity at Yalta had now been fulfilled. In early April Churchill learned that these leaders had disappeared.

None of this seems to have dented Roosevelt's belief in Stalin's good intentions or in their resolve to share the partition of Europe with the Soviets. On returning from Germany Churchill heard that instead of taking Berlin, now less than 100 miles from the Allied front line, Eisenhower proposed leaving Berlin to the Russians and switching the US armies towards Leipzig and Dresden while the British and Canadians pressed north for Hamburg, and had communicated this information directly to Stalin. Once again Churchill protested; once again his protest was ignored.

'The idea of neglecting Berlin and leaving it to the Russians to take at a later stage does not appear to me correct,' he wrote to the CCS on 31 March. 'As long as Berlin holds out and withstands a siege, as it might easily do, German resistance will be stimulated. The fall of Berlin might cause nearly all Germans to despair.' Nothing happened; the Red Army, having raped its way across East Prussia was now to rape its way into Berlin.

With the Rhine frontier breached by the US, Canadian, French, and British Armies, the Germans were already in despair, not least because the Russian Armies now stood on the doorstep of the Reich and were thirsting for revenge. Given the choice, Germany would surrender Berlin to the Western Allies, as quickly as possible but no action was taken before President Roosevelt died on 12 April.

Churchill found this news, 'a very painful, personal loss, quite apart from the ties of public action which bound us together' and made immediate preparations to fly to the funeral. In the end he was obliged to stay in Britain where he made a glowing tribute to the late President in the

House of Commons on 14 April – 'he had brought his country through the worst of perils and the heaviest of toils. Victory had cast its sure and steady beam upon him.'

Churchill now had to form a new relationship with the new President, Harry S Truman. He quickly discovered that Truman had no ingrained political agenda, was not the man to be pushed around by the Russians, and was equally determined to stand up to Soviet demands. The problem was that this resolve came too late – on 8 May, 1945, the war in Europe ended, with the Russians firmly in control from Berlin and all across Europe to the east and south east into Poland, Czechoslovakia, Romania, Albania and beyond; the Communists would not be dislodged from their control of this territory for another fifty years.

The end of the war in Europe called forth another burst of Churchillian oratory, much of it inspired by the tremendous ovation he received whenever he appeared in the streets of Britain or in Parliament, a tumult of praise and gratitude summed up in a letter from the Foreign Secretary, Anthony Eden on 8 May, 'All my thoughts are with you on this day, which is essentially your day. It is you who have led, uplifted and inspired us through the worst days. Without you, this day could not have been'

No one who lived through the Second World War would disagree with that.

The war was not over. Japan still had to be dealt with and the war in the Far East was waged with great ferocity in Burma and the Pacific, by sea and land, until the dropping of the two atomic bombs on Hiroshima and Nagasaki in August finally brought the war to an end on 15 August, 1945, almost six years after Germany invaded Poland – and Poland was still troubling Churchill, not least because of what its subjugation to the Soviets meant for the rest of Europe.

On 13 May, Churchill expressed his fears in a BBC broadcast to the British people:

'I wish I could tell you', he said, 'that all our toils and troubles are over...and if you thought you had had enough of me and I ought *to be put out to grass, I tell you I would take it with the best grace...but I have to tell you there is still a lot to do.'*

'On the Continent of Europe we have yet to make sure that the simple and honourable purposes for which we entered this war are not brushed aside or overlooked in the months following our success. There would be little use in punishing the Hitlerites for their crimes if law and justice did not rule and if totalitarian or police govern- ments were to take the place of German invaders.'

Churchill was not able to play a major part in this post-war task, for in July he was dismissed from office by the British public – a major blow to Churchill and a great surprise to almost everyone else.

Churchill, as already related, had wished the Coalition to con- tinue, certainly until the defeat of Japan, possibly until well into the peace. His Labour colleagues in the Coalition, Attlee, Bevin and Morrison, were at first inclined to go along with this suggestion but the Labour Party in the country thought otherwise. At their annual conference the party members demanded an immediate election – the first for ten years – and a resumption of Party politics. This resolution brought down the Coalition Government and on 23 May Churchill went to see the King at Buckingham Palace and resigned. The King then asked him to form a Caretaker Government until elections could be held and the votes of soldiers overseas counted. This was done and the elections for a new Parliament took place on 5 July.

It cannot be said that Churchill handled the election campaign well. He did particular harm to his election prospects on 4 June by alleging in a BBC election broadcast that the Socialists could only rule *'with the help of a Gestapo,'* a comment insulting to his former Labour colleagues in the Coalition and one which Attlee, the Labour Party leader, dismissed with contempt.

Churchill also claimed that many of the proposals in the Beveridge Report were either premature or too expensive. Although the general opinion was that Churchill could not lose, it is now hard to see how that confident opinion was arrived at, other than by basing all Tory election hopes on Churchill's wartime reputation.

These hopes were misplaced. The country and the soldiery wanted that better world they had been waiting and fighting for and they did not trust the Tories to deliver it. Even before 1945, the Tories had been losing seats at every by-election to the middle-of-the-road Commonwealth Party, the latter filling in as opposition as the Coalition electoral pact prevented any Labour candidates from standing. This evidence was ignored as was a mass of anecdotal evidence

When Churchill asked the chief of Bomber Command, Air Marshal Harris, how his men would vote, Harris replied that 80 percent of them would vote Labour. When Churchill commented that then 20 per cent would vote Tory, Harris replied '*No, sir, twenty per cent will not vote at all.*' Newspaper opinion polls also confirmed that there would be a Labour landslide, but in spite of all the evidence, most individuals and almost all the MP's assumed that Churchill would remain in office. The UK polling day was set for 5 July but the result would not be announced for another three weeks, to allow time for the overseas soldiers vote to be taken and counted.

Before the election results could be announced there was another major conference between the Powers held at Potsdam, close to Berlin on 15 July. Given the pending announcement of the election result, Churchill took the Labour leader Clement Attlee with him and at Potsdam Churchill and Attlee met Truman for the first time. They also heard that the atomic bomb which had just been tested in the Nevada desert had exploded successfully, without destroying the planet as some scientists had feared. Churchill also visited Hitler's former Chancellery – '*tracking the Beast to its lair*' as he put it – and apart from a number of lavish banquets, attended a splendid Victory Parade in Berlin. Attlee accompanied him to this event and observers noted that the cheers for the Labour leader coming from the soldiers were louder and longer than those for Winston Churchill.

The Potsdam Conference had the task of setting up the United Nations and establishing the rules for the government of Germany in the immediate future. Churchill was equally determined to get the future of Poland on the agenda as well. Churchill got on well with the new President but the old disputes still lingered. The President agreed that the CCS should continue to function but the US Joint Chiefs then came back to insist that while they were happy to discuss matters of general strategy with the British, any decision on subsequent action would be taken by the US Chiefs alone, a view which made any continuation of the wartime CCS arrangement a waste of time.

Nor was there much satisfaction on the Polish issue; Stalin continued to claim that free elections had been held and insisted that while Russia continued to hold Polish land in the east, up to the so-called Curzon Line, the Poles were at liberty to take over land in East Germany and redraw the frontier to place over twenty percent of German territory inside Poland – yet another cause for yet another war. No argument prevailed on Stalin – the new western frontier of Poland would be on the rivers Oder and Neisse, less than 100 miles from Berlin.

Stalin did receive one setback at Berlin, and a traumatic one. He had been told nothing of the atomic bomb and the news of this terrible weapon, once explained to him by his scientists, came as a most unpleasant surprise. No longer would massive armies be the deciding factor in the world's power struggles; the arbiter of events would be the nation, or nations, that possessed this new device, and for some years that meant only the US and Great Britain. This news did not lead to Stalin softening his approach or releasing the Communist grip on Poland or the other East European countries, but any ambitions for futher gains in Western Europe seem to have been put on hold.

The UK election results were due on 25 July and Churchill and Attlee were both obliged to return to Britain, the victor coming back to Potsdam two days later as the sole UK delegate. Stalin and Truman both expected that Churchill would return and when Churchill landed in London he was told that the Conservative Party were projected to win with a majority of around 70 seats. That happy prospect quickly vanished on the morning of 26 July when the first results came in; Labour had captured ten solid Tory seats.

Two hours later, before Churchill sat down to lunch, it was clear that there was going to be a Labour landslide. The Conservatives lost 372 seats and Labour came to power with a majority over all other parties of 146 – a crushing blow for Churchill, in spite of Clementine's kindly comment that the result might well prove to be *'a blessing in disguise.'* This remark did nothing for Churchill's mood. *'At the moment all I can say is that it seems quite effectively disguised,'* was all he could reply.

12. The Final Years

1945 - 1965

'He was the greatest Englishman of our time –
I think the greatest citizen of the world of our time.'

Clement Attlee, 1965

When the Second World War finally ended with the surrender of
Japan on August 15, 1945, Winston Churchill was seventy years old,
out of office, and very tired. The war years had taken their toll of his
health, and although Churchill did not see it that way at the time, his
loss of power in the 1945 election may indeed have been a blessing in
disguise. Apart from providing him with the opportunity for a much-
needed rest, it provided the time to rebuild his shattered personal
finances.

This is not to say that Churchill neglected either his Parliamentary
duties or his role as Leader of the Opposition in the immediate post-
war period; far from it. As at many other times in his long political
career, he may have been out of office but he was not out of the public
eye, and his presence now was exalted by the reputation established
during the wartime years. Even during the 1945 election, many people

tempered their determination to elect Socialist Government with the regret at losing Mr Churchill. Once out of office his popularity was immense.

Moreover, this was a time when Churchill's voice was needed. The country had voted for a change in direction but a gradual one; the wish was to retain the best of the old and incorporate the necessary changes with it to create a better, more egalitarian society. Many Labour politicians, on the other hand, saw their majority as a mandate for total change and intended to change the nature of British society, root and branch; the possibilities for social conflict were immense. The problems of peace turned out to be hardly less difficult than the problems of war.

Just to begin with, Britain was broke. Lend-Lease was abruptly cancelled as soon as the war ended and Britain then had to negotiate a massive, crippling, multimillion dollar loan from the US simply to buy food. Wartime austerity continued and even intensified; to stay financially afloat Britain would have to keep the belt tight for years. Bread, freely available during the war, went 'on ration' when the war ended so that grain supplies could go to the starving populations of Europe. Food rationing regulations remained in Britain until 1952, seven years after the war.

The root of Britain's problem was that her politicians still wished to play a major role in world affairs, a position Britain no longer had the means or the energy to support. This policy was short-sighted and had the opposite effect to the one intended. Efforts and finance that should have been devoted to restoring Britain's industrial base, and thus her political clout, was spent on maintaining vast forces overseas and in creating the Welfare State. The end result was chronic weakness, political, industrial and financial, and in attempting to secure the end of social justice without thought of the means, the Labour Party were laying up trouble for decades ahead.

While these troubles were getting under way Churchill was taking that well-earned rest. Having absorbed the shock of the election results he remained in Britain until Parliament assembled in August. The

Second World War ended two weeks later and in early September Churchill went off for a painting holiday in Italy and the South of France, leaving Clementine to start work refurbishing Chartwell, which had been closed during the war years, and was in sore need of redecoration. She also moved into their new London home at Hyde Park Gate which would remain Churchill's home for the rest of his life. Basking in the warm sunshine of the Italian Lakes and the Riviera, he spent a great deal of time painting and began to relax, writing to Clementine that:

> 'It has done me no end of good to come out here and resume my painting... The Japanese war being finished and complete peace and victory assured, I feel a great sense of relief which grows steadily; others have to face the hideous problems of the aftermath – it may all indeed be a blessing in disguise.'

To say that he enjoyed this bout of long-overdue relaxation is not to imply that Churchill was entirely happy with his removal from the centre of affairs. Labour's willingness to dispense with the Empire, the problems of Eastern Europe, the relentless Soviet stranglehold on Berlin and Austria, were areas where he felt that all his previous efforts had been brought to nothing and his warning voice gone unheard. The term 'Iron Curtain' used widely later to describe the Soviet barrier to contact between Eastern Europe and the free world, comes into his correspondence at this time – and reappeared when in 1946 he accepted an invitation from President Truman to visit the US and give a lecture at Westminster College in Fulton, Missouri.

Churchill accepted with pleasure; travelling was always one of his great pleasures and he was much in demand, not least in newly liberated Europe where his speeches and wartime efforts have never been forgotten. A visit to France and Belgium in November 1945 turned into a triumphal progress as his car drove through streets crammed with cheering people and he was offered the freedom (honorary citizenship) of a dozen cities. In Brussels he made a speech calling for a United States of Europe, a term that has since provided much comfort to Europhiles, though it is clear that he meant a union of independent states and not a European Federation under bureaucratic central control. On retuning to England he was awarded the Order of Merit by King George VI and a few days later he sailed for the US. Arriving in New York, he took the train at once for the beaches of Florida, arriving there on 16 January and spent a few days basking in the sunshine and public admiration.

Churchill had maintained close contacts with the United States since his first visit decades ago, and the main purpose of this 1946 visit was to deliver two or three speeches to the alumni of Westminster College at Fulton, Missouri – Missouri being the home state of President Harry Truman; the invitation had come to Churchill via the President's office. Churchill was glad to escape a cold winter with its rigours for a few weeks in Florida, some enjoyable chats with his American friends and, most of all, to make what he intended as a keynote speech at Fulton. The President himself conducted Churchill there, Truman having offered to introduce Churchill to the alumni and make the opening address.

Fulton is a small town, far removed from the political hothouse of Washington or London, but Churchill decided that it would provide the ideal Anglo-American platform from which he could speak out about the current state of the world, the rising dangers of Communist subversion, and what could and should be done about it. This 'Iron Curtain' speech, as it came to be called, marked a return to the very best Churchillian rhetoric and took the theme that the cause of all the current ills affecting the free world was the continuing and growing Communist threat – and the solution was some form of Anglo-American alliance.

'From Stettin in the Baltic to Trieste in the Adriatic, an Iron Curtain has descended across Europe. Behind that line lie all the capitals of the ancient states of Central and Eastern Europe. Warsaw, Berlin, Prague, Vienna, Budapest, Belgrade, Bucharest, and Sophia,

*all these famous cities and the populations around them lie in what
I must call the Soviet sphere, and all are subject, in one form or
another, not only to Soviet influence but to a very high and, in many
cases increasing measure of control from Moscow. Athens alone –
Greece with its immortal glories – is free to decide its future at an
election under British, American and French, observation.'*

'This,' Churchill added,'*was not the liberated Europe we fought
to build up. Nor is it one which contains the essential of permanent
peace.'*

Churchill's speech was neither aggressive nor jingoistic but it
caused a considerable stir in the US and Soviet Russia and much
comment, not all of it favourable. Churchill did not think that Soviet
Russia wanted war – *'only the fruits of war and the indefinite expansion
of their power and doctrine'* – and suggested that the only answer to this
expansion was the creation of a strong Europe, the firm hand of the
United Nations, and a close alliance between the British Commonwealth and the US, *'in fraternal association.'* Inevitably this 'Iron
Curtain' speech, delivered to the massed US media and in the presence
of the US President, attracted a great deal of attention in political and
diplomatic circles.

Churchill had shown Truman a draft of this speech during their
train ride to Missouri. According to Churchill, the President had
approved of both the contents and the tone, telling Churchill that the
expression of these sentiments could do nothing but good. However,
when some US newspapers began to criticise the contents – the *Wall
Street Journal* commenting that, *'The United States wants no alliance, or
anything that resembles an alliance with any other nation'* – Truman gave
a press conference at which he denied ever seeing a draft of the Iron
Curtain speech. Overall, the American reaction to the Iron Curtain
speech was lukewarm at the time; only later did the US press and
politicians begin to regard it as a clear statement of the situation,
offering a way out of a growing dilemma.

In his Fulton speech, Churchill reminded the audience of the rise of Fascism in the 1930s, of which he had warned:

> '...*my own fellow countrymen and the world but no one paid any attention'. There never was a war in the whole of history easier to prevent without the firing of a single shot and Germany might be powerful, prosperous and honoured today. But no one would listen and one by one we were all sucked into the awful whirlpool. This must now be allowed to happen again.'*

Unfortunately, history has a way of repeating itself and no one would listen at Fulton either. Churchill's warnings of the late 1940's were no more heeded than those of the 1930's. What saved the world from another war, this time with Communism, was not the resolution of the free world but the atomic and hydrogen bomb. The dawning consequences for the planet should these ever be deployed did not halt the development of nuclear weapons. Then came nuclear proliferation and a peace secured by relying on nuclear terror, all resulting from a failure of unity and resolve. What Churchill wanted was a display of resolution among the democratic nations; what was on offer was a constant temporising with Soviet aggression and the build-up of a United Nations organization that would provide little more than endless opportunities for endless discussion.

Evidence that Churchill was right in what he said at Fulton is provided by the reaction of Stalin, who described Churchill as a '*warmonger,*' a man '*anxious to sow the seeds of discord between the Allied Governments and make collaboration difficult.*' Collaboration was not on offer from the Soviets and the Cold War that began in 1945 was to continue for another forty-five years until the Soviet Union collapsed.

Undaunted by this barrage of press criticism, Churchill moved on to his next speaking engagement in Virginia and repeated his call for a '*union of hearts among the English-speaking peoples, based on conviction and common ideals.*' Before leaving New York at the end of his visit in

March, Churchill gave a final speech in which he answered his critics both in the US and Russia:

> *'I have never asked for an Anglo-American military alliance or a treaty. I have asked for something different and in a sense I asked for something more. I asked for fraternal association – free, voluntary, fraternal association and I have no doubt that it will come to pass, as surely as the sun will rise tomorrow.'*

Churchill may not have asked for a military treaty in 1946 but in the end one was created, the North Atlantic Treaty Organisation – NATO – a defensive organization founded on the principle that an attack on one free nation was an attack on all. NATO came into existence in 1949 and provided a bulwark against Communist aggression and expansion in Western Europe until the Berlin Wall came down in November 1989.

In spite of these initial criticisms, the Fulton speech did nothing but good. In speaking out about Soviet intentions, Churchill gave voice to what many people were thinking. Once these issues had been brought into the open, they could not be locked away again. Churchill's speech showed the Free World exactly what it was up against with the Communist threat and when this threat manifested itself later in 1947, when the Russians closed the Berlin Corridor in an attempt to force the Western contingents out of Berlin, the West was already mentally prepared. As a result they were quickly able to summon up a steadfast response: the Berlin airlift of 1947-1948, which supplied the city with all it needed to survive until the Russians. Realising they could not starve the city into surrender and that the West was not going to abandon the Berliners, Stalin re-opened the land corridor.

On his return to the UK Churchill encountered the old problem – money. Churchill stood to make a fortune from his war memoirs but they were not yet written. He had earned next to nothing during the war and received no gratuity on leaving office. The most immediate problem was his much-loved country home at Chartwell, which needed considerable expenditure at once to be liveable after five years of neglect but which Churchill felt unable to maintain.

This problem was ended by a proposal from an old friend, Lord Camrose. He suggested that if Churchill would agree to donate Chartwell to the Nation on his death as a memorial to his life and work, then Camrose would raise sufficient funds to purchase the house, on the understanding that the Churchills could live in it until his death and pay only a 'peppercorn' rent of £350 ($1400) a year. Having consulted Clementine, Churchill accepted this proposal, adding that the contents of the house would also be left as a gift to the nation – an action which, with Camrose's initial proposal, has resulted in Chartwell remaining as a splendid shrine to Churchill's memory, carefully maintained by the National Trust.

All this took a little time – the eventual purchase price, together with the necessary endowment for upkeep of the property, came to around £100,000 ($400,000), a very substantial sum in 1946 – the present-day value being in the region of £2 million (say $3 million at the present rate of exchange). Churchill was so bemused by these figures that he offered cheerfully *to throw in the corpse as well,'* but by the time Chartwell's future was settled Churchill's finances had greatly improved. The sums received by the sale of his memoirs and various other works and copyrights brought him in a most substantial sum, sufficient to live out his life in great comfort and still leave a fortune to his wife and children.

When staying at Chartwell about this time, Churchill had a curious experience. He had converted a small cottage in the grounds into a studio and – or so goes the story - one afternoon in November 1947, when he was painting a copy of a portrait of his father, he felt that he was not alone. Turning round, Churchill saw his father sitting in an armchair,' *looking just as I had seen him in his prime.'*

This sudden apparition does not seem to have disturbed or even surprised Churchill; he took it rather as a rare chance to have a long-wanted conversation with his much loved parent and bring his father up to date with his life in politics and three hard wars he had fought since 1895.

This conversation did not, apparently, lead Lord Randolph to appreciate just how well his son had done in the last fifty years. *'We fought two great wars and won them,'* said Winston, *'with the help of our allies,'* but Lord Randolph did not enquire into what part, if any, his eldest son had played in these exploits. On the contrary, Lord Randolph, or his ghost, seemed quite convinced that Winston was now either a retired military man or a portrait painter though, Lord Randolph conceded, having inspected the copy, quite a good one.

'I never expected that you would develop so far and so fully,' he told Winston. *'But when I hear what you say I am really surprised that you did not go into politics....you might even have made a name for yourself.'* With that comment, Lord Randolph's shade vanished and never reappeared. This story is related in Martin Gilbert's *Churchill: A Life,* but was apparently first recounted to his children, who referred to it later as The Dream. Dream or not, Churchill appears to have enjoyed the experience, or perhaps just the rare opportunity of a few words of private conversation with his father.

Less congenial were Churchill's exchanges with another wartime partner, General Charles de Gaulle, who took grave exception to Churchill's 1947 proposal that France *'should take Germany by the hand and rally her to the West and European co-operation'* – a suggestion which, said de Gaulle had been badly received in France – but had in fact been badly received by de Gaulle. Churchill had endured a great deal from this tiresome Frenchman during the Second World War – *'The worst cross I had to bear,'* he once said ruefully, *'was the Cross of Lorraine,'* referring to the wartime symbol of de Gaulle's Free French.

In spite of Britain's generous support of France and the Free French during the war, perhaps even because of it, de Gaulle was a rabid Anglophobe. When France and Germany, with four other European nations, got together to form the European Economic Community (EEC) in the 1950's, de Gaulle saw to it that Britain was excluded – and Britain did not in fact join the EEC until after de Gaulle died.

Apart from painting and travelling, leading the Opposition in the House of Commons and keeping up his contacts with leading world figures, Churchill's main occupation during the time out of office from 1945-1951 was filling a number of highly lucrative literary contracts, beginning with his multi-volume work, *The Second World War*, essentially his wartime memoirs, for which he received $1.4 million for the US rights alone, with further substantial sums from British newspapers and book publishers. To produce this book Churchill retained a number of secretaries and research assistants and the six volumes came out at regular intervals from June 1948, long hours of work at Chartwell being interspersed with painting holidays in Marrakesh, the South of France, or Madeira.

Meantime, the Labour Government of Clement Attlee was running the country and disposing of the British Empire, doing neither in a way that attracted much support from Churchill. He approved the National Service Act in 1947 which introduced a two-year period of military service for all British males between the ages of 18-26, but disapproved of the rapid pullout from India in the same year, saying that it would lead, as it did, to the rapid winding up of the British Empire. Rather than prolong the agony, Churchill and the Conservative Party did not oppose the Indian Independence Bill when it passed through Parliament and led to the establishment of India and Pakistan – and a dispute over Kashmir that has yet to be resolved. Other independence bills followed, the next one for Burma.

The Tories were far more critical and vocal over the various nationalisation bills Labour were introducing into Parliament – bills for public ownership of the railways, coal mines, and steel mills. When these bills were brought before the House, Labour's large majority made any resistance futile. Neither was Churchill any more successful in rousing opposition against further Communist moves in Eastern Europe, especially in early 1948 when the Czech Communist Party seized power in Prague.

Britain was far more interested in getting out of Palestine where the British Mandate ended in May 1948. This was after many British soldiers had been killed attempting to keep the peace between the two communities – and after a great deal of carping from the US. This last so irritated Churchill that it provoked him into pointing out that if the Americans were unhappy about the way Britain was handling Palestine, perhaps the best solution was to take the task on themselves. *'I am not aware that any advantage had ever accrued to Britain from this painful and thankless task,'* said Churchill, *'and someone else should have their turn now.'*

Naturally no other nation, not even the US, was anxious to take on the thankless and costly task of mediating between Arabs and Jews. The British departed on 14 May, 1948 – and the first Arab-Israeli war broke out just 24 hours after British troops left the port of Haifa.

Churchill was now 74 years old, and although he retained much of his old zest and was working hours that might have worn out a much younger man, there were some doubts on how long he could continue to do so. There were quiet calls for a successor, notably his long-time heir-apparent, Anthony Eden. Clementine for one felt that enough was enough and that he should retire gracefully and let Eden play himself in before the next election in February 1950.

Churchill decided to hang on until then and was considerably disappointed when the Labour Party remained in power after the election, albeit with a much-reduced overall majority of just six seats. Although the Socialists could look forward to support from the nine Liberal members, it was more than likely that another General Election would be needed in the near future, certainly before the end of the usual five-year term. This being so, Churchill again chose to remain as Leader of the Conservative Party in the Commons and celebrated that decision – one not universally well received within the Parliamentary party – with some powerful speeches in the House. These included a ringing endorsement of the Government's decision to send British forces to Korea when the North Koreans invaded the South in June 1950.

Labour stayed in power into 1951. Churchill, now 76, continued to work on his wartime memoirs until October 1951, when Attlee decided to call a General Election – Churchill's sixteenth election since he had first stood for Parliament before the South African War of 1899. Polling day was 25 October and the result was a Conservative victory by 321 seats to Labour's 295, hardly a landslide but more than sufficient to last a five-year term.

Churchill's first decision at the first Cabinet meeting was to denationalise steel and reduce Ministerial salaries by 30 per cent. The country's economic position was still perilous and Churchill felt that the Government had to set an example – and then extended these economies by launching an all-out attack on Government spending. Another equally pressing problem, obvious to others but one he chose to ignore, was Churchill's age and growing infirmity. When he reached his 77th birthday in November 1951 he was growing decidedly deaf and while still vigorous, at least for a man of his age, he was not the man he had been when last in office.

Churchill declared that he intended to stay in office for one year and then give way to a younger man and set out to make his last year busy and productive. In January 1952 he went to New York and Washington for discussions with Truman over the Korean War and NATO. That done, he made a two-day visit to Ottawa before returning to Washington to address both Houses of Congress. This speech was largely devoted to the Middle East, including the problems of the Suez Canal which the Egyptian Government wished to take over from Franco-British control and the continuing problems between Israel and the Arabs. He returned to England on 28 January, a week before King George VI died of cancer.

Churchill, born a Victorian, had now lived long enough to enter the reign of another monarch, Elizabeth II. He became fully determined to stay in office for her Coronation in the following year. but his increasing feebleness and inability to cope with the demands of public life – even making a speech now tired him out – was now clear to everyone. This included some Socialist MP's in the House of Commons who did not hesitate to taunt Churchill on his deafness, a cruel and unedifying spectacle to all who remembered Churchill during the

Second World War. However, the situation could not continue; in June 1952 a group of senior Tories called formally on the Prime Minister and asked Churchill either to resign or set a date for resignation.

Before giving a positive answer to this appeal, Churchill took another long holiday in the South of France, followed by the Prime Minister's traditional visit to the Sovereign's Scottish home at Balmoral. He still declined to say when he would resign and continued to find reasons to stay on, the next being in November 1952 with the election of Dwight D. Eisenhower as US President. Eisenhower was Churchill's old colleague in wartime days, so Churchill was among the first to congratulate the new President by telephone. In January 1953, to the chagrin of his ministerial colleagues, he went to Washington for talks.

Anthony Eden, the heir-apparent, was convinced by now that death alone would drive Churchill from Downing Street. The death of Stalin in March 1953 seemed to confirm an equal dedication in Winston Churchill, to hang on until the end. However, by now the hints that he must go – rather than merely should go – were coming in thick and fast. These hints included his latest honour as Knight of the Garter, coveted membership of an Order of Chivalry dating back to the reign of Edward III in the 14th century, a great mark of Royal esteem but a hint nevertheless.

Elizabeth II was crowned on 2 June, 1952, and on 23 June Churchill suffered a stroke. The effects worsened over the next few days and by 27 June Churchill was partially paralysed. Another meeting with Eisenhower in Bermuda was postponed and a statement was issued to the Press, saying that Churchill needed a complete rest. Though barely able to speak, Churchill still declared that he would recover from this setback and fully intended to address the Conservative Party Conference in October.

The story of Churchill's life during these last months in office is a triumph of will over adversity. He recovered from the worst effects of the stroke by sheer determination and spent much of his 'complete rest' working on the final volume of his Second World War memoirs – and was indeed able to make that address to the Party Conference in

October. This event was followed by another signal honour, the award of the Nobel Prize for Literature.

Demands for his resignation, if only for his own sake, continued to grow inside Parliament and the Party. They were taken up by the Press in February 1954, continued throughout the year – and were largely ignored. Whether Churchill was right to cling on to power is at best debatable. The true verdict is probably not, though he could still show flashes of his old skill with words. An example of this came in 1954 when, replying to an address, he gently declined the credit for the late victory:

> 'It was the nation, and the race dwelling all round the Globe that had the lion's heart. I had the luck to be called upon to give the roar. I also hope that I sometimes suggested to the lion the right place to use his claws.'

Churchill was still coping – just – with the demands of public life and his most obvious successor, Anthony Eden, was also in poor health. As Churchill saw it, there was still a lot to do and he still had some considerable influence in world affairs. All that is true, but sooner or later he would have to retire and it might have been better for Churchill and any eventual successor if he had gone sooner and let the new man play himself into the post before the next General Election. Finally, in December 1954, Churchill told Eden he would retire the following April – six months before the Prime Minister must call a General Election – and this time he kept his promise.

On 4 April Churchill gave a formal dinner at Downing Street for the Queen and the Duke of Edinburgh. On the following day he held a final Cabinet meeting at which he thanked them all for their support over the years and gave them a final piece of advice – 'never be separated from the Americans.'

That done, he drove to Buckingham Palace and submitted his resignation to the Queen. She offered him a dukedom – he was offered the title Duke of London – Her Majesty having previously ascertained that Churchill would decline. This he did, stating that he preferred to stay in the House of Commons as Sir Winston. That done, Churchill left for a painting holiday in Sicily and Anthony Eden became Prime Minister.

Churchill returned to the House of Commons in April 1955 and in the subsequent election saw the Conservatives returned to power. He retained his seat and appeared in the House from time to time but spent most of the following summer working on another major book, his *History of the English Speaking Peoples*. He now found relief in giving up the burdens of office – aged 89 – writing to Eisenhower in 1955 that, *'I did not know how tired I was until I stopped working,'* though he was still working hard at constituency business and on his books.

In the following year Britain became involved in her last imperial adventure, a dispute over the Egyptian seizure of the Suez Canal, then owned by the British and French. This led to allegations of collusion with Israel and a Franco-British attack on Egypt, Operation Musketeer, a landing at Port Said. President Eisenhower, who blocked Britain's oil supplies and ordered the sale of sterling to provoke an economic crisis in the UK, eventually stopped this venture. There were many other problems in Europe at this time, most notably the Hungarian uprising against the Soviets in Budapest that was put down by the Russians with great brutality, but the Suez debacle marked the end of Britain as an imperial power. From now on the retreat from Empire speeded up and by the mid-1960s it had gone.

Churchill was a strong supporter of the Suez operation, stating that Israel was in danger and that Arab ambitions in the Middle East had to be curbed. He believed that the landings and the subsequent advance down the Canal would have demonstrated resolve in the face of Arab aggression but realised the risks both of undertaking the operation and the consequences of failure. A few weeks after the British withdrawal, Churchill said to an adviser, who asked what he would have done in Eden's place, *'I would never have dared to do it – and if I had dared I would never have dared to stop.'*

Churchill believed that Eden's action was right but premature; the Western interest in the Middle East, largely based on concern over oil supplies, was under attack from both Communism and Arab nationalism. Churchill believed that the latter would prove the decisive factor and one which had to be tempered by showing the Arabs that the West had interests in the region and would defend them, with force if need be. This lesson was not learned at the time and had to be learned again in 1990-91 and 2002-03 in the subsequent conflicts with Iraq. In 1956 matters worked out otherwise; very ill and broken-hearted, Eden resigned after Suez and was replaced by Harold Macmillan, who undertook the task of repairing relations with the United States.

Churchill's last years represent a gradual dimming of the light. He faded gently from the political scene, still rallying to speak in public from time to time, devoting much of his time to painting and seeing those old friends who were still alive. Other signs of age – growing deafness and recurring short bouts of illness – made increasingly frequent appearances.

Churchill had now been taken up by the Greek shipping millionaire, Aristotle Onassis, who took him on regular winter cruises on his yacht and generally looked after him but in 1963, during a visit to Monte Carlo, Churchill fell and broke his hip. After treatment and a short convalescence in Britain, Churchill returned to Monte Carlo and another cruise with Onassis but was back in England again by July when he suffered yet another stroke.

This time he did not recover. Although he made occasional public appearances and dined with old friends at home, he was now in his own private world for much of the time. His long and active life was drifting quietly to a close. The end came in January 1965 when, now aged 91, Churchill suffered another massive stroke. He lingered for two weeks and died at home in London on 24 January, 1965, a Sunday – exactly 70 years to the day after the death of his father.

Churchill had already written out the arrangements for his funeral, stating that he wanted 'lots of bands.' The British have the knack and the experience for such occasions and all the majestic ceremonial the Nation could provide was brought out in salute.

Churchill's body lay in state in Westminster Hall for three days; more than 300,000 people filed past by night and day to pay their last respects. The body was then taken through the streets of the city, the pavements crowded with mourners, the military bands playing the slow marches Churchill wanted, and so into St Paul's Cathedral. Here Nelson and Wellington, two other British heroes, had been laid to rest in the previous century and here the nation gathered for Churchill's funeral service. Six thousand people attended, including the Queen of England, five other sovereigns, and fifteen Presidents or Prime Ministers.

That done, the coffin was taken down to the river Thames by a naval party and carried upriver on a launch, the dockyard workers bowing their cranes in respect as it passed by. And finally, later on that bleak winter day, Winston Churchill returned to his birthplace at Blenheim and was laid to rest in the little churchyard at Bladon, next to his brother Jack and both his parents ad there, far from the noise and bustle of his busy life, his journey came to an end.

Over the decades since his passing, Churchill's reputation had grown rather than diminished – as is usual with most great men. Perhaps this is because so many of his prophecies have come to pass and his foresight is now recognized. Perhaps it is because he was the outstanding example of a democratic political leader. More probably, his reputation is sharply illustrated by comparing him with the lesser lights that have come to power in the world since his passing.

What can be said with certainty is that he was the last in a distinguished line of truly world-class statesmen – in my view *the* greatest statesman of the 20th century. Since Churchill's death, no one in public office anywhere has come within a light year of his style and breadth of vision; the world may never look upon his like again.

13. Bibliography

The bibliography on Winston Churchill is extensive, with at least 500 biographies of various kinds available and more being written all the time. What follows is a list of titles the author found most useful in preparing this brief work. Those who wish to continue studying Churchill's life and times have plenty of works to call on.

Direct quotations from parliamentary speeches and debates can be found in *Hansard*, which is The British Parliament's Official Report of proceedings in the House of Commons and Lords. Citations from the War Cabinet meetings can be found in *The Cabinet Office to 1945*, published by the UK Public Records Office.

The author would urge anyone interested in a deeper study of Churchill's life and career to read some of the books listed here but concentrate on reading the books written by Churchill himself, most of which are still available in public or university libraries or in paperback editions.

Addison, Paul, *Churchill on the Home Front*, London, 1992.

Ashley, Maurice, *Churchill as Historian,* London, 1968.

Blake, Robert, *Winston Churchill*, London, 1998.

Bonham-Carter, *Churchill as I Knew Him,* London, 1965.

Brown, Anthony, *Long Sunset,* London, 1995.

Calder, Angus, *The People's War, Britain, 1939-1945,* Cape, London, 1969.

Churchill Randolph and Gilbert, Martin. *The Churchill Biography, Complete in Eight Volumes from 1874-1965, London, 1980.*

Churchill, Winston. S. *My Early Life,* Butterworth London, 1930.

Churchill, Winston S. *The World Crisis, 1911-1918,* (2 Vols) London, 1938.

Churchill, Winston, S. *The Second World War,* (6 vols.) Cassell, London, 1949-52.

Colville, John, *Footprints in Time,* London, 1976.

Enright, Domininique, *The Wit of Winston Churchill,* London, 2001.

Gilbert, Martin, *Churchill: A Life,* London, 1991.

James, Robert Rhodes, *Churchill: A Study in Failure,* London, 1970.

Jenkins, Roy, *Churchill,* London, 2001.

Jablonsky, David, Churchill: *The Great Game and Total War,* London, 1991.

Lewin, Ronald, *Churchill as War Lord,* London, 1973.

Moran, Lord, Winston Churchill: *The Struggle for Survival,* 1966.

Parker, Robert, *Winston Churchill: Studies in Statesmanship,* London, 1995.

Roberts, Andrew, *Eminent Churchillians,* London, 1994.

Sandys, Celia, *Churchill: Wanted, Dead or Alive.* London 1999.

Soames, Mary, *Churchill: An Unruly Life,* London, 1994.

Stafford, David, Roosevelt and Churchill, London 1999.

Wheeler-Bennett, John, and others, Action this Day: Working with Churchill, London, 1968.

Index

INDEX